THE BRITISH LIBRARY
writers' lives

Elizabeth Barrett Browning and Robert Browning

MARTIN GARRETT

THE BRITISH LIBRARY

THE BRITISH LIBRARY
writers' lives

Elizabeth Barrett Browning
and Robert Browning

XLIII

How do I love thee? Let me count the ways.—
I love thee to the depth & breadth & height
My soul can reach, when feeling out of sight
For the ends of Being and ideal Grace.
I love thee to the level of everyday's
Most quiet need, by sun & candlelight—
I love thee freely, as men strive for Right;—
I love thee purely, as they turn from Praise:—
I love thee with the passion, put to use
In my old griefs;... and, with my childhood's ~~the childhood's~~ faith.—
I love thee with the love I seemed to lose
With my lost ~~Saints~~ Saints!— I love thee with the breath,
Smiles, tears, of all my life!—and, if God choose,
I shall but love thee better ~~after~~ death.

~ Contents

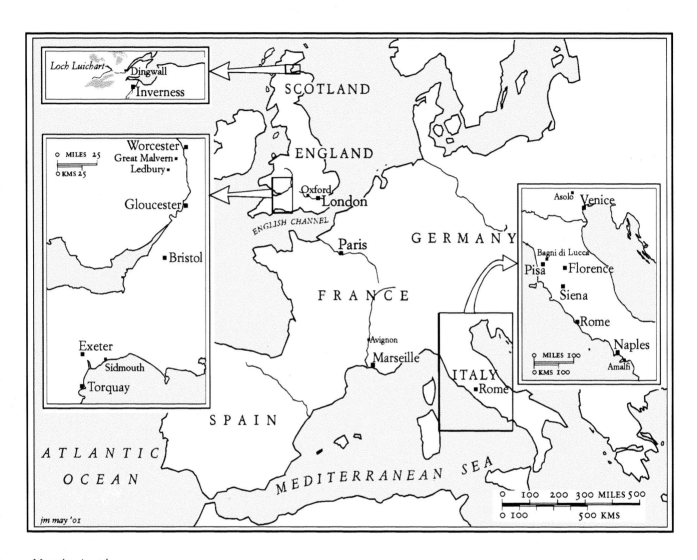

Map showing places associated with the Barrett Brownings.

≋ *Elizabeth Barrett*

The Barrett family amassed its wealth, in the late eighteenth century, with the aid of slave-workers on sugar plantations in the British colony of Jamaica. The poet's father, Edward Moulton-Barrett, was born there and later directed the business and estates from London. Mary Graham-Clarke, whom he married in 1805, came from a family long known to his own and with similar commercial interests. Their daughter Elizabeth well understood the consternation of owners when slaves were emancipated by parliamentary act in 1833, but rejoiced for humanity. Although her family in fact treated their slaves unusually well, guilt was one factor in the love of liberty – whether for slaves, child-workers, women, or nations – which her poems often declare.

The child whose full name was, a little awkwardly, Elizabeth Barrett Moulton-Barrett, was born on 6 March 1806 at Coxhoe Hall, near Durham. 'Ba', as

Coxhoe Hall, the birthplace in 1806 of Elizabeth Barrett Moulton-Barrett. The hall was demolished in 1952 because of mining subsidence.

Photograph c. 1900 by courtesy of Harry Holder

her family called her, was the first of twelve children, all but one of whom survived infancy. In 1809 the growing family moved to Hope End (a 'hope' is an enclosed valley), near Ledbury in Herefordshire, where Edward Barrett converted the original house into stables and built a splendid new mansion in exotic 'Turkish' style. In this house, with its extensive grounds, Elizabeth Barrett spent an active, largely happy childhood. As yet there was little sign of the fearsome tyrant whom her father later became in the eyes of several of his children and of posterity. Father and sons played cricket. Indoor amusements included short plays which the precocious Elizabeth wrote and acted in with her brother Edward ('Bro', born 1807), her sister Henrietta (born 1809) and other siblings. Both parents were enthusiastic supporters of her early writing. In 'Glimpses into My Own Literary Character', a manuscript essay written when she was fourteen or fifteen, Barrett remembered how 'in my sixth year' (actually she was nine)

> *For some lines on virtue which I had penned with great care I received from Papa a ten shilling note enclosed in a letter which was addressed to the* Poet Laureate of Hope End; *I mention this because I received much more pleasure from the word* Poet *than from the ten shilling note – I did not understand the meaning of the word* Laureate, *but it being explained to me by my dearest Mama, the idea first presented itself to me of celebrating our birthdays by my verse.* 'Poet Laureate of Hope End' *was too great a title to lose.*

My dear Mama
I love you very
much. & I hope you
love me. I hope you
like kinnersley.
we have been very
good, Brakas just told
me how England

is bounded & has done
it very well. tell dear
Papa the Rusians
has beat the french kill'd.
18.000 men & taken
14000 prisners. Bro &
Hen meo & Sam joins
with me in love to Papa
& you & John your dear
august 31.t   Ba

Many of these birthday odes to her parents and siblings survive. Although not particularly remarkable poetry, they are good apprentice-work for one who soon came, she says in 'Glimpses', to long for poetic fame and to see literature as 'the star which in prospect illuminated my later days…the spur which prompted me, the aim, the very soul of my being'.

Fortunately, Barrett did not simply dream. She soon realized that such fame could be achieved only by dint of wide reading and determined application. From a very early age, initially under her mother's guidance, she read widely in English literature. A keen interest in languages also helped to extend her imaginative experience. She started to learn French when she was six or seven and Latin and Greek not long afterwards. By the end of 1816 she had progressed far enough with French to compose a short French classical tragedy, *Régulus*, for herself, Bro and Henrietta to perform. (One of the soliloquies was, she recalled, concocted in her

Letter from Elizabeth Barrett to her mother, written at the age of six on 31 August 1812. Contrary to what Barrett says in the letter, the Russians did not, in fact, 'beat the French' at the Battle of Smolensk.

The British Library Add. MS 60575 ff1,1v

'house under the sideboard'.) What to many children would be hard labour was sheer excitement as far as the young poet was concerned: 'poetry and Essays were my studies and I felt the most ardent desire to understand the learned languages. To comprehend even the Greek alphabet was delight inexpressible.'

A classical education was the traditional – and traditionally male – requirement for anyone wanting to become established as a serious poet, but few girls were offered such an opportunity. That girls almost never learnt Greek was, for the ambitious Elizabeth, part of its appeal. She persuaded her father to allow her to learn the language with Bro, who was being prepared by his tutor, Daniel McSwiney, to go away to school at Charterhouse. Within the immediate family there seems to have been no suggestion that her interests were eccentric or unbecoming for a female, or that she should be sewing or playing the piano (which she disliked) instead. In 1842 she told her friend Mary Russell Mitford that her only concession to 'the duties belonging to' what she calls 'my femineity' was that, amid much pricking of fingers and knotting of thread, she

> *once knitted an odd garter, and embroidered an odd ruffle, and committed fragments of several collars, and did something mysterious, the name of which operation has past from my head, towards producing the quarter of a purse, and made several doll's frocks, and one or two frocks for a poor child of mine adoption.*

It is difficult to say why this particular nineteenth-century family, later remembered for the authoritarian attitudes of its father, should have been so enlightened in this respect. The fact that Barrett was, as she goes on to say to Mitford, 'always insane about books and poems – poems of my own, I mean, and books of everybody's else', obviously helped. Her evident enthusiasm, ability and strength of will met with encouragement rather than resistance from her loving parents.

By the age of twelve she was writing short novels and plays, translating, and experimenting with different sorts of poetry. *The Battle of Marathon*, her long poem on the ancient 'war of Greece with Persia's haughty King', was privately printed, at her father's expense, for her fourteenth birthday in 1820. Life now, however, began

in some ways to become more difficult. In April 1821 all three Barrett sisters were ill with headaches and convulsions. Henrietta and Arabel (born 1813) soon recovered, but Elizabeth did not. In July she also developed measles, and afterwards was sent to recover at the Spa Hotel, Gloucester. Here she remained for about ten months, while doctors disagreed on diagnoses and treatments. She complained of a swollen spine and was suspended for some time in a contraption known as a 'spine crib'; this, together with the then-common belief that sick women must rest absolutely, probably weakened her further. Perhaps she did suffer from an unidentified illness, perhaps it was partly psychosomatic, but it became established that she must rest and that she needed to take opium. (This, administered in the alcoholic tincture laudanum or as morphine, was commonly prescribed for many illnesses at the time; the problem of addiction was not yet properly understood.) Having successfully resisted well-meaning doctors' attempts to curtail her reading and writing, she began to send work to periodicals, first achieving publication with 'Stanzas…on the Present State of Greece' – the Greek war for independence from the Turkish empire had just begun – in the *New Monthly Magazine* in May 1821. Her ambitious poem *An Essay on Mind* was finished in the spring of 1825 and published a year later.

Barrett already had an appreciative family audience, but *An Essay on Mind* brought her the wider and more critical response she craved. Uvedale Price, a distinguished classical scholar known to her parents, read the poem and began corresponding with her. Flatteringly, he sought her opinion of his nearly finished work on the pronunciation of Latin and Greek; he accepted many of her suggestions and remained in fruitful contact with her until his death in 1829. It was during the time she was in dialogue with Price that the first signs of disharmony with her usually encouraging father appeared. On 4 February 1827 she wrote an untitled private description of her feelings when Edward Barrett was less than appreciative of her poem 'The Development of Genius'. To her amazement, he found the first few pages of the poem, which she had laboured over for months, illegible, obscure, too inexplicit and lacking in variety. To him the hero of the poem was an insufferable madman and the verse unharmonious:

> *Indeed the whole production is most* wretched*! I must tell you so – and I think*
> *it is quite lamentable that you should have passed so much time to such an*
> *effect. You see the subject is beyond your grasp – and you must be content*
> *with what you can reach. I cannot read any more – I would not read over*
> *again what I have read for ten pounds – really not for fifty. I advise you to*
> *burn the wretched thing.*

She felt 'mortified' and 'grieved'. It seemed 'a little hard that half an hour of patient attention should not be vouchsafed to my half year's patient composition'. Price, she noted, had responded positively to the poem.

It is easy to read too much into this incident. Certainly father and daughter had periods of close and evident affection afterwards. She felt great sympathy for his situation when her mother died, unexpectedly, of rheumatoid arthritis in 1828. But the 'Development of Genius' affair shows one potential area for tension. Edward Barrett was perhaps irritated less by the details of the poem than by a sense that his daughter's interests were moving away from his own, that she now needed him less than in childhood and adolescence. She still cared greatly about his reactions – 'Papa would be sorry to think how much he grieved me!' she concludes, half-lovingly, half-bitterly – but she increasingly tended to seek the opinion of friends, such as Price, the blind scholar Hugh Stuart Boyd who first wrote to her a month after the 'Development of Genius' incident, or, later, her fellow writer Mary Russell Mitford.

Great Malvern in Worcestershire. Barrett stayed here with her friend Hugh Stuart Boyd and his family in the spring and autumn of 1830.

The British Library 10352 e11

All three were considerably older than she was, and each acted as a substitute, to a certain extent, for her lost mother and decreasingly idealized father.

Boyd lived with his wife and daughter at Malvern Wells and for a time at Great Malvern, a few miles from Ledbury. Unlike Price, Boyd was unknown to the Barretts before the correspondence began, so Elizabeth Barrett had difficulty in convincing her father that it was proper, and herself that she had the courage, to meet him. When she eventually did, in the spring of 1828, they focused on their main common interest: Greek. Over several years she read Greek literature to him, and learned much about it from him. But her diary of 1831–32 reveals that her relationship with Boyd was more emotionally troubling to her than he can ever have known. She talks of her uncertainty about how much her friend and mentor likes her, of her uneasy encounters with his wife and daughter, her jealousy of other young women who visit him, and her fury at herself for harbouring such feelings. It was her first experience of emotional involvement outside the family – a belated experience for one whose adolescent years had been spent reading, writing, being ill and pleasing her parents.

Something else for Barrett to worry about in 1831–32 was whether her family would soon be leaving the beloved Hope End. There had been financial anxieties since 1824, when a protracted lawsuit involving the inheritance of property and slaves in Jamaica from Edward Barrett's grandfather had ended in a decision against him and his brother Samuel and in favour of their cousins the Goodin-Barretts. The Moulton-Barretts remained wealthy, but not as extraordinarily wealthy as they had been. One of the consequences of this was the eventual sale of Hope End in 1832. Both before and after the sale Edward Barrett failed to discuss his worries and his decision with his children. To some extent he simply fulfilled a common nineteenth-century notion, supported on the whole by religion, of loving but commanding and rather remote fatherhood. But to some extent too his own nature was lonely and intransigent; his daughter – looking back, it is true, from the perspective of her own disenchantment with many aspects of his character – told Browning that her mother had 'a sweet, gentle nature, which the thunder [her father's difficult side] a little turned from its sweetness – as when it turns milk'.

Extract from Barrett's 'The Seraphim' (1838), a dialogue between the angels or 'mystic beings' Zerah and Ador.

The British Library Ashley MS A211 f111

The Barretts moved to Sidmouth on the Devon coast in August 1832 and then to London – 74 Gloucester Place in December 1835 and 50 Wimpole Street in April 1838. The poet continued to publish widely. In 1838 the publishers Saunders & Otley brought out *The Seraphim, and Other Poems,* her first work under the name Elizabeth B. Barrett rather than EBB. The ambitious title-poem – too ambitious for the taste of most reviewers – concerned, she told her friend and distant relation John Kenyon, 'the supposed impression made upon angelic beings by the incarnation and crucifixion – a very daring subject'. Her religious poems usually addressed such less 'daring' topics as 'A Sabbath Morning at Sea'.

Most readers found the 'Other Poems' more accessible than *The Seraphim*. Many of these had first appeared in periodicals, such as the *New Monthly Magazine* and the prestigious *Athenaeum*. One of the *Athenaeum* poems suggests most interestingly the direction of much of her later work: 'The Poet's Vow' is a ballad in which a (male) poet separates himself from his fellow human beings, having 'vowed his blood of brotherhood/To a stagnant place apart'. He rejects Rosalind, his intended bride, along with everyone else; he expects that she will simply agree to marry his friend. At first she, in traditional female fashion, can only try, grievingly, to remind him of their childhood together and his mother's dying wish that they should marry. He remains unmoved, but Rosalind has the last word. When she dies, her old nurse, as instructed, takes her body to the would-be inhuman poet, together with an emphatic message which jolts him back to fellow-feeling:

> *Look on me with thine own calm look -*
> *I meet it calm as thou!*
> *No look of thine can change* this *smile,*
> *Or break thy sinful vow.*
> *I tell thee that my poor scorned heart*
> *Is of thine earth…thine earth, a part -*
> *It cannot vex thee now*
>
> *…I charge thee, by the living's prayer,*
> *And the dead's silentness,*
> *To wring from out thy soul a cry*
> *Which God shall hear and bless!*

Otherwise she may stand 'pale among the saints…[a] saint companionless'. Since this breaks the poet's heart – and his foolish vow – she is 'Triumphant Rosalind'. In a sense the woman has found, in death, a voice; she has much more to say for herself, for instance, than the Lady of Shalott, floating dead to her would-be lover in Tennyson's poem of 1832, which Barrett knew and admired. Women had rarely been allowed such a voice, whereas in Romantic poetry – written by men – it was

*Mary Russell Mitford
(1787-1855), play-
wright, author of
country stories, and
Barrett's most valued
correspondent before she
met Browning. Portrait
by John Lucas in
coloured chalk, 1852.*

*National Portrait Gallery,
London*

acceptable, indeed desirable, for a poet to seek silent, lofty communion with nature like Rosalind's unkind lover.

Several of Barrett's ballads were written to accompany illustrations in *Findens' Tableaux*, an annual publication with a mainly female readership. This was edited by Mary Russell Mitford, whom she met in May 1836. Mitford was a well-established literary figure, best known for her tales of country life, *Our Village*, published between 1819 and 1832. Her writing career had been driven by the need to support her charming, extravagant and quite unreasonable father. For some years the letters between Barrett and Mitford were a lifeline for both women – a place to discuss and recommend other authors by the dozen, to share an enthusiasm for French literature, to talk about their work, plans and family situation. Mitford was impressed by Barrett's learning, but also by her physical presence. Her beauty, she told a friend a few years later,

One of Barrett's drafts for 'Psyche Apocalypté', the verse drama which she considered writing, in collaboration with R.H. Horne, in 1840-41.

The British Library Ashley MS A2518 f8

Vol. ─   Act III

Scene I

Mountains peering upon luxuriant plains beneath.

Enter Medon & the child.

They advance with hurried steps ─ but Medon knows not where he is going. He is only flying from Psyche ─ into nature. They pause for breath. The child's voice speaks for (interprets the voice of) nature, and is echoed by Psyche invisibly. Medon starts forward again ─ and stops suddenly by a form half covered with the drifted snow. It is the dead body of his abandoned bride, Enore.

The child falls upon its knees ─ & buries its head in the cold snow of the cold bosom of white death. Medon starting erect with anguish, calls upon Psyche to appear. He will fly no more ─

Psyche appears .

Medon restored & strong by the reason of strong woe, is able to look upon & confront Psyche.

Scene II

A lofty forest vista, like a cathedral.

In the centre a new made grave, surrounded by Islanders.

Chorus of Islanders.

(The earthliness of death ─
The sorrow of the blind
that see only the worm─)

The body of Enore borne in attended by Medon & the child, with Psyche visibly hovering over them .

proceeded from contrasts – a slight, girlish figure, very delicate, with exquisite hands and feet, a round face, with a most noble forehead, a large mouth, beautifully formed, and full of expression, lips like parted coral, teeth large, regular, and glittering with healthy whiteness, large dark eyes, with such eyelashes, resting on the cheek when cast down; when turned upward, touching the flexible and expressive eyebrow; a dark complexion, with cheeks literally as bright as the dark China rose, a profusion of silky, dark curls, and a look of youth and of modesty hard to be expressed.

Elizabeth Barrett was becoming steadily better known in the literary circles of which London was the focus. But from the autumn of 1837, her health began to decline once more, and she was confined to her room by a succession of severe coughs and colds. Obviously there was some kind of problem with her lungs. Her doctor was satisfied that she did not have tuberculosis, one of the main killers of the century, but strongly advised her to leave London for a warmer place. In August 1838 her father sent her to Torquay on the Devon coast. She was accompanied by various members of the family and visited, when possible, by her anxious father. Bro, still her dearest companion, would have been sent to work in Jamaica, having found no other occupation in life, had she not pleaded with her father to let him stay with her in Torquay. In consequence, irrationally but understandably, she blamed herself, when, in July 1840, Bro, three friends and a boatman were drowned while sailing, in seemingly perfect conditions, in Tor Bay. Barrett was seriously ill for several months. Her mind seemed 'broken up into fragments'. For the rest of her life she talked as little as possible, even to her husband, about what had happened. For a time she was 'miserably upset' when, without her permission, Mary Mitford saw fit to explain to the public, in her *Recollections of a Literary Life* (1852), 'the fatal event which saddened her bloom of youth'. Barrett remained in Torquay, with its terrible associations, until she finally persuaded her father to let her travel back to London, by slow stages, in the autumn of 1841.

Mitford is undoubtedly right in her *Recollections* to say that the main reason for Barrett's recovery was the 'wholesome diversion' of literature and Greek. She was also helped by her strong religious faith and by Mitford's gift – much better judged than her later revelations – of Flush, a cocker spaniel, son of her own dog of the same name. By the end of 1840, while still physically frail, Barrett was in correspondence with the writer and traveller Richard 'Hengist' Horne about his earlier proposal that they should collaborate on a verse drama. Within a year this project had petered out, but Barrett got as far as producing some interesting fragments of the play, which at her suggestion was to be called *Psyche Apocalypté* ('the revealed soul'), and was led into some equally interesting discussions in her correspondence with Horne: 'the terror attending spiritual consciousness…seems to admit a certain grandeur and wildness in the execution', she wrote to him in January 1841; 'There are moments when we are startled at the footsteps of our own Being, more than at the thunders of God.' Such

Elizabeth Barrett with her spaniel, Flush, 12 December 1843, in a drawing by her brother Alfred. (The pleasant view through the window is imaginary.) Virginia Woolf's Flush *(1933) tells the Brownings' story from the dog's point of view.*

Eton College, Windsor

reflections were perhaps sharpened by the inner pain she had experienced following Bro's death; this, says Mitford, 'gave a deeper hue of thought and feeling, especially of devotional feeling, to her poetry'.

Back in Wimpole Street, Barrett worked hard on poetry, both devotional and secular. Her extensive and intelligent prose studies – *Some Account of the Greek Christian Poets* and *The Book of the Poets*, an account of English poetry since the Middle Ages – were serialized in *The Athenaeum* in 1842. (She earned £20 for *The Book of the Poets*, and at once offered it to Mitford, who was, as usual, in financial difficulties because of her father, but politely refused.) Barrett's two-volume collection of *Poems* (1844) was widely and mostly favourably reviewed. It contains a number of pieces, such as 'The Cry of the Children', written at least partly in response to Mitford's encouragement, as expressed in a letter of October 1841, to write more 'poems of human feelings and human actions. [These poems] will be finer, because truer, than any "Psyche" can be.'

'The Cry of the Children' was first published in *Blackwood's Edinburgh Magazine* in August 1843 as a reaction to the findings of government commissions on the employment of children in factories and mines; one of the official reports was written by Horne. The reports made clear that conditions were often so appalling – children as young as five were working long hours for low wages using dangerous, noisy machinery – that death seemed a pleasant alternative. In the poem 'Little Alice died last year', Alice's fellow workers, looking into the pit dug for her grave, notice that there is 'no room for any work in the close clay'; listening by the grave they hear no crying, and 'Could we see her face, be sure we should not know her,/ For the smile has time for growing in her eyes'.

Perhaps this seems too simply sentimental for modern readers, but the poet's aim is to give the children a voice – a voice more passionate than could be expressed in the official reports – just as she gave a voice to Rosalind in 'The Poet's Vow' or to the abused black speaker of her later anti-slavery poem 'The Runaway Slave at Pilgrim's Point'.

Barrett explored social inequality in a different context in 'Lady Geraldine's Courtship', completed at some speed when her publisher, Edward Moxon, requested an extra piece to make the two 1844 volumes equal in length. The poem was, the author wrote to Hugh Stuart Boyd, 'a romance of the age' – a contemporary work which explores the love between an earl's daughter and a well-known but socially inferior poet. Lady Geraldine's guests laugh at the poet (Bertram) or look askance at him. They are insincere, the women's voices 'low with fashion, not with feeling'. But Geraldine chooses for herself. To the poet's great surprise she reciprocates his love, choosing him as one 'Very rich in virtues, – very noble'. Soon afterwards Barrett herself would accept the advances of a man of whom her father disapproved – although it was clear that he would have disapproved of any possible suitor.

LADY GERALDINE'S COURTSHIP.   225

And the river running under; and across it, from the
                rowans,
A brown partridge whirring near us, till we felt the
                air it bore,—

There, obedient to her praying, did I read aloud the
                poems
Made by Tuscan flutes, or instruments more various,
                of our own;
Read the pastoral parts of Spenser—or the subtle
                inter-flowings
Found in Petrarch's sonnets—here's the book—the
                leaf is folded down!—

Or at times a modern volume,—Wordsworth's solemn-
                thoughted idyl,
Howitt's ballad-~~dew~~ *verse*, or Tennyson's enchanted re-
                verie,—
Or from Browning some " Pomegranate," which, if cut
                deep down the middle,
Shows a heart within blood-tinctured, of a veined
                humanity!—

VOL. I.   Q

Extract from Barrett's corrected copy of 'Lady Geraldine's Courtship' (1844) for her Poems (1850). The poem's praise of Browning prompted his first letter.

Appropriately, Robert Browning first wrote to Barrett partly in response to a comment in 'Lady Geraldine's Courtship', where Bertram reads his lady poems including 'from Browning some "Pomegranate", which, if cut deep down the middle,/Shows a heart within blood-tinctured, of a veined humanity'. (Browning published his work between 1841 and 1846 under the collective title *Bells and Pomegranates*, intended to suggest 'an alternation, or mixture, of music with discoursing, sound with sense, poetry with thought'.)

The modern theme and setting of 'Lady Geraldine' have affinities with the contemporary novel as much as with poetry. And it was on the whole among novelists, rather than poets, that Barrett found examples of serious, successful women predecessors and contemporaries. Her immediate predecessors, the poets Felicia Hemans and 'LEL' (Letitia Elizabeth Landon), struck her as having failed to break away from a traditionally 'feminine', rather unadventurous field of reference. Among female novelists, by contrast, there was a shining light in the person of George Sand (the pen name of Aurore Dudevant), who dared to explore social and sexual issues, combining, as Barrett put it in a sonnet published in 1844, the best attributes of either sex: 'Thou large-brained woman and large-hearted man,/Self-called George Sand!' But in poetry, as she wrote to the critic Henry Chorley in January 1845, 'I look everywhere for grandmothers and see none. It is not in the filial spirit I am deficient, I do assure you – witness my reverent love of the grandfathers!'

In writing her most important poem, *Aurora Leigh*, on an epic scale, she would be following and, for all her reverence, challenging, the tradition of the 'grandfathers'; in writing sonnets, she had already entered one male preserve. Her ability to commence a work on this scale was helped by the steady improvement of her health from 1843 onwards. Even before she knew Browning, she was becoming stronger, allowing a few more outsiders to see her after years of restricting contact mainly to correspondence. The art historian and feminist Anna Brownell Jameson (1794–1860), for instance, first visited her at the end of 1844 and Barrett also saw John Kenyon quite often. Although she still kept to her comfortable but rather dark room in Wimpole Street, she was even becoming interested in the idea of going to Italy. While marriage would open new worlds and themes to her, she was not, in 1845, a frail invalid waiting to be rescued – as legend and sometimes her own imaginings would have it – but an ambitious poet with plans for the future.

Following pages:

Robert Browning knew London well from childhood onwards and returned to it as his permanent base in 1861. Elizabeth Barrett lived in the city in 1835-38 and 1841-46 and began to see much more of it when her health improved in the summer of 1845.

Holborn viaduct looking east by Thomas Shotter. Guildhall Library, Corporation of London

~ *Robert Browning*

Robert Browning was born in Camberwell, south London – then a village outside the city – on 7 May 1812. He enjoyed a close relationship with both his parents. 'Since a child,' he told Elizabeth Barrett in June 1846 – three months before he finally left the parental home to go to Italy with her – 'I never looked for the least or greatest thing within the compass of their means to give, but given it was.' They gave him liberty, he said, and they trusted him. His mother, Sarah Anna Wiedemann (1772–1849), of partly German descent but herself from Dundee, was remembered by her fellow Scot, the social critic and historian Thomas Carlyle, as 'the true type of a Scottish gentlewoman'. She was devout, keen on music, animals and gardening, and the centre of a close-knit family, consisting of herself, her husband, their son, and their daughter, Sarianna (1814–1903).

Robert Browning Senior (1782–1866) had experienced less happy relations with his own family. As a young man he had been sent by his father (yet another Robert Browning) to work on the Caribbean island of St Kitts, where his mother's family had plantations. But, unlike the Barretts, Mr Browning Sr found that he could not tolerate working in a system reliant on slave labour. In disgust at the slaves' treatment, Browning explained to Barrett in 1846, he 'relinquished every prospect, – supported himself, while there, in some other capacity, and came back, while yet a boy, to his father's profound astonishment and rage'. He thought of a career as an artist, but his father refused to support him and so he found instead, through a St Kitts connection, a steady, reasonably well-paid job as a clerk at the Bank of England, where his father was a more senior (and less popular) official. In his spare time he pursued his artistic bent as an amusing and

The only known likeness of Robert Browning's mother, Sarah Anna, drawn by her husband, Robert Sr., who in his spare time was a prolific caricaturist.

Wellesley College Library, Special Collections

prolific caricaturist. He also amassed, and encouraged his son to read widely in, a vast library: history, classics, essays, philosophy, early editions of poetry, the French *Biographie universelle* (1822). When the family moved to a larger house at New Cross, a few miles south of Camberwell, in 1840, the book collection filled most of the third storey.

Learned and unusual references – often found abstruse by readers and reviewers – came naturally to Browning from this background. As well as reading in his father's library and discussing with him what he read, Browning frequently visited Dulwich Picture Gallery, near Camberwell; art and artists would often figure in his poems. And there was also music: he played the piano and cello, sang, and occasionally composed, probably mostly in his teens. Another interest shared with his mother was animals. His friend Alexandra Orr records in her *Life and Letters of Robert Browning* (1891) how as a young child

> *he would refuse to take his medicine unless bribed by the gift of a speckled frog from among the strawberries; and the maternal parasol, hovering above the strawberry bed during the search for this object of his desires, remained a standing picture in his remembrance.*

Later 'he kept his owls and monkeys, magpies and hedgehogs, an eagle, and even a couple of large snakes'. (Orr's source for this material was either Browning himself or his sister.)

Like his future wife – even more so, probably – he benefited from a remarkably secure family background. Unlike her, he wrote little poetry in childhood, although he did remember that he 'extemporized verse aloud while walking round and round the dining-room table supporting himself by his hands, when he was still so small that his head was scarcely above it'. Later, at about fourteen, he compiled *Incondita*, a volume of verse heavily influenced, like much writing of the day, by the work of Lord Byron. Only two of the poems have survived, and these only because they were copied out by a friend of the family, Sarah Flower. She was a poet herself and her elder sister, Eliza, became well known as a composer and performer of (mainly religious) music. Through the Flowers, Browning met

William J. Fox, a well-known Unitarian minister and writer, who tactfully persuaded him to burn *Incondita* rather than trying to publish it. As far as is known, he desisted from writing poetry for some time after this, but not from reading it. Soon after *Incondita* he discovered Shelley's poetry, and it was under Shelley's influence that he became, an atheist or, at least, a doubter. This position was temporary; by the early 1830s he was attending not only his parents' Congregational church but also the Anglican Camden Chapel. In the longer term, although he opted out of organized religion, he remained on the whole a believer. Browning's enthusiasm for Shelley was, however, longer lasting – the main evident influence on his next venture into poetry, *Pauline* (1833).

Pauline followed experiments in other directions. After leaving Peckham School in 1826, he had studied, at or from home, subjects including fencing, dancing, drawing and boxing. In 1828 he became a student at London University (now University College, London), recently established for the benefit of those excluded from Oxford and Cambridge on the grounds of religion: all those from denominations other than the Church of England. (One thing Barrett and Browning had in common was their Dissenting background.) His father recommended him on the grounds of his moral trustworthiness and 'his unwearied application, for the last six years, to the Greek, Latin and French languages'. But conventional study was not, it seems, to his liking; at the end of the first year Browning Sr. wrote again to register his son's 'painful' and 'unexpected' decision to withdraw. Nevertheless, parental support – moral and financial – continued. Mindful of his own father's contrasting attitude, the poet's father exerted little or no pressure on him to find a career. Browning continued his education, reading yet more, learning Italian, probably writing verses we know nothing about, and becoming an enthusiastic theatre-goer who went to see both Edmund Kean, the decaying but still sometimes fiery great actor of the Romantic period, and the younger, more sober and more authoritative William Charles Macready.

Pauline, according to Browning, originated indirectly from a theatre visit. On 22 October 1832 he went to the King's Theatre, Richmond, to see Kean, in one of his last appearances, as Shakespeare's Richard III. Inspired by the

acting, and perhaps also by Richard's chameleon skills and superbly successful deceptions, Browning came away from the theatre excitedly conceiving what he later called

> *a foolish plan…which had for its object the enabling me to assume and realise*
> *I know not how many different characters; – meanwhile the world was never*
> *to guess that 'Brown, Smith, Jones and Robinson'…the respective authors of*
> *this poem, the other novel, such an opera, such a speech, etc. etc. were no other*
> *than one and the same individual.*

The University of London, now University College London, where Browning studied unhappily from October 1828 to May 1829. It was founded in 1826; the building shown here, designed by William Wilkins, was completed in 1828.

The British Library 08365 k27

Pauline: a Fragment of a Confession, published with the aid of £30 from a kindly aunt in 1833, was intended to be 'the first work of the Poet of the batch'. This scheme

Alfred Domett (1811-87), self-portrait, c1830-40. He was one of Browning's closest friends until 1842, when he emigrated to New Zealand, where he later became prime minister. After Domett's return to England in 1872 Browning encouraged him to publish his long New Zealand poem 'Ranolf and Amohia'.

The British Library AC 1342 d(3)

shows the scope of the young man's ambition. More importantly for his future writing, it provides early evidence of his fascination with different roles, masks and identities. His experience of these was, thanks to gender, opportunity and disposition, greater than Elizabeth Barrett's. He went to the theatre and to social gatherings, he became part of a lively and intelligent group of friends who called themselves 'the set', and in 1834 he even travelled through northern Europe to St Petersburg as part of the entourage of the Russian consul general in Britain. Social life also gave him the opportunity to develop his lifelong interest – much stronger than Barrett's – in clothes and fashion. William Fox's daughter Eliza remembered him, at a time when she was about sixteen and he was twenty-six, as 'slim and dark, and very handsome; and – may I hint it – just a trifle of a dandy, addicted to lemon-coloured kid gloves and such things'. Fine clothes, a touch of dandyism, were another mask to play with.

'The first work of the Poet' is the restless, anguished confession of a young speaker uncertain in love, religion and poetry. To some extent it is autobiographical, certainly more so than most of Browning's poems – he was still looking for a place in the world, for a style and an identity. Nevertheless, the poem is the utterance of a speaker, addressed to an evidently fictional Pauline; there is a tradition that she was inspired by Eliza Flower, whom Browning first knew in his teens, when she may have been his music teacher, but the woman in the poem is hardly individualized at all. In subsequent Browning monologues listeners will matter more, subtly conditioning and interpreting the speaker's words.

This first, anonymous publication sold not a single copy. The author told his

sister about it but not his parents, perhaps because of the autobiographical elements, perhaps out of simple fear of disappointing them through failure, and he later revised and reprinted it with reluctance. Yet it helped, in its small way, to launch Browning's career by bringing him once more to the attention of William Fox, with whom he had lost contact after *Incondita*. Fox felt that the poet had made progress since that early attempt, and reviewed *Pauline* in the periodical he owned and edited, *The Monthly Repository*, as 'evidently a hasty and imperfect sketch' but one which 'gave us the thrill, and laid hold of us with the power' of genius.

Between 1834 and 1836 *The Monthly Repository*, which had a reputation for advanced thinking in politics, religion and art, published several shorter poems by Browning. These included, in January 1836, his first really distinctive monologue,

The following Poem was written in pursuance of a foolish plan which occupied me mightily for a time, and which had for its object the enabling me to assume & realize I know not how many different characters;—meanwhile the world was never to guess that "Brown, Smith, Jones, & Robinson (as the Spelling-books have it) the respective authors of this poem, the other novel, such an opera, such a speech &c &c were no other than one and the same individual. The present abortion was the first work of the Poet of the batch, who would have been more legi =mately myself than most of the others; but I surrounded him with all manner of (to my then notion) poetical accessories, and had planned quite a delightful life for him:

Only this crab remains of the shapely Tree of Life in this Fool's paradise of mine.

RB

PAULINE.

PAULINE, mine own, bend o'er me—thy soft breast
Shall pant to mine—bend o'er me—thy sweet eyes,
And loosened hair, and breathing lips, and arms
Drawing me to thee—these build up a screen
To shut me in with thee, and from all fear;
So that I might unlock the sleepless brood
Of fancies from my soul, their lurking place,
Nor doubt that each would pass, ne'er to return

The opening of Pauline *(1833), Browning's first published work.*

Victoria & Albert Museum, London

'Porphyria' (later called 'Porphyria's Lover'). Here the speaker explains, with chilling logic, how his beloved, who had 'vainer ties' to someone else, tried to comfort him, spreading over him her yellow hair; and so he knew at last

Porphyria worshipped me; surprise
Made my heart swell, and still it grew
While I debated what to do.
That moment she was mine, mine, fair,
Perfectly pure and good: I found
A thing to do, and all her hair
In one long yellow string I wound
Three times her little throat around,
And strangled her.

The killer sits on with her: 'And all night long we have not stirred,/And yet God has not said a word!' No more has the poet, who refrains, to powerful effect, from comment. Only hints are dropped: a repeated reference to her shoulder and head as 'it' not only shows that she is dead but suggests the speaker's objectifying of her; only dead can she fulfil his longings and remain, in a grimmer sense than usual, the object of his desire. Porphyria's silence in the poem, alive and dead, speaks eloquently of

An extract from 'Porphyria's Lover', originally called 'Porphyria: a killer's monologue'.

The British Library 012200 de8/10

LYRICS

PORPHYRIA'S LOVER   85

Her hat and let the damp hair fall,
   And, last, she sate down by my side
And called me. When no voice replied,
She put my arm about her waist,
   And made her smooth white shoulder bare,
And all her yellow hair displaced,
   And, stooping, made my cheek lie there,
And spread o'er all her yellow hair,   20
Murmuring how she loved me ; she
   Too weak, for all her heart's endeavour,
To set its struggling passion free
   From pride, and vainer ties dissever,
And give herself to me for ever :
But passion sometimes would prevail,
   Nor could to-night's gay feast restrain
A sudden thought of one so pale
   For love of her, and all in vain ;
So, she was come through wind and rain.   30
Be sure I looked up at her eyes
   Proud, very proud ; at last I knew
Porphyria worshipped me ; surprise
   Made my heart swell, and still it grew
While I debated what to do.
That moment she was mine, mine, fair,
   Perfectly pure and good : I found
A thing to do, and all her hair
   In one long yellow string I wound
Three times her little throat around,   40
And strangled her. No pain felt she ;
   I am quite sure she felt no pain.
As a shut bud that holds a bee
   I warily oped her lids ; again
Laughed the blue eyes without a stain.

Por-
phyria's
love and
death

how she personally has been left out of the speaker's considerations. And although the poem is grouped in *Dramatic Lyrics* (1842) under the heading 'Madhouse Cells', the madman does not rave. He is terribly calm, not a stage madman but one seen from inside. Like the speakers of so many later Browning poems he is to be justified, or condemned, seemingly from his own mouth.

It was not such short pieces, however, which introduced Browning to literary London, but the long poem *Paracelsus* (1835), in which a figure based loosely on the sixteenth-century physician and alchemist Paracelsus grapples with idealism and its limitations, perfect love and human imperfection. This, the first work published under Browning's own name, attracted good reviews in such prominent periodicals as *The Examiner*. The general tone of the comments is perhaps best summed up by William Charles Macready's private impression – in his diary entry for 7 December 1835 – of 'a work of great daring, starred with poetry of thought, feeling and diction, but occasionally obscure; the writer can scarcely fail to be a leading spirit of his time'.

Even without *Paracelsus* and its reception, Browning would perhaps have obtained an invitation for the supper party after the successful first night of Thomas Noon Talfourd's play *Ion* at Covent Garden Theatre on 26 May 1836. But it was because of *Paracelsus* that Talfourd proposed a toast to him as 'the youngest poet of England' and William Wordsworth declared, 'I am proud to drink your health, Mr Browning.' (Two days later Wordsworth met the older and somewhat more established Miss Barrett.) The previous month Browning had met Thomas Carlyle, who was still calling him 'little Paracelsus Browning' in a letter to a friend of 1842. Carlyle was soon taking a keen, if sternly critical, interest in his work post-*Paracelsus*. And Macready, who had starred in *Ion* and was the most important (sometimes self-important) actor of the day, delighted Browning by suggesting that the young poet might like to write a play for him.

With Macready and the theatre, Browning began a long and often difficult relationship. The friendship foundered ultimately on their demanding personalities and the unbridgeable gap between poetic ideas and ideals and the practicalities and audience preferences of nineteenth-century theatre. Macready felt drawn to Browning's 'simple and enthusiastic manner...; he looks and speaks more like a youthful poet' – he was nearly twenty years Macready's junior – 'than any man I ever saw'. The 'youthful poet' now launched into writing a historical tragedy about the downfall of Thomas Wentworth, Earl of Strafford, adviser to King Charles I. Macready read the first version of *Strafford* in November 1836 and made many suggestions about how to make it more stageworthy. So began a long saga, recorded in the actor's diaries, of re-readings and re-writings, the author by turns excited and 'jaded and thought-sick', spats and reconciliations and the complicated, fluctuating relationship between the actor, the playwright and John Forster (1812–76), the influential friend of Browning and Dickens, who acted effectively as go-between. Macready saw the main problem early on, identifying in March 1837 both the play's virtues and its lack of commercial viability: 'Read Strafford in the evening, which I fear is too historical; it is the policy of the man, and its consequence upon him, not the heart, temper, feelings, that work on this policy, which Browning has portrayed – and how admirably.' At times Macready wished Browning would withdraw the work, or delay longer, but he felt that he should press on out of loyalty and out of admiration for the work's literary (rather than theatrical) qualities. He was flattered – and forced to go on, perhaps – when the poet asked permission to dedicate to him the printed text of the play.

Eventually *Strafford* was given four performances at Covent Garden, with Macready in the title role, in May 1837. It was more enthusiastically received than the actor had expected; quite enough for Browning to continue along what with hindsight seems a wrong turning by writing more plays. Relations between actor and poet declined markedly. In August 1840 Browning turned up, Macready's diary records, 'before I could finish my bath, and really *wearied* me with his obstinate faith' in the value of his own works; 'I fear he is for ever gone.' *The Return of the Druses*, the play they were debating this time, struck Macready as

William Charles Macready (1793–1873), the foremost tragic actor of the1830s and1840s and manager of Covent Garden Theatre (1837–39) and of Drury Lane (1841–43). His diary is a useful source of information on early Victorian theatre. He put on two of Browning's plays, but lost his friendship in the process.

The British Library 1560/884

Covent Garden Theatre, where Browning's play Strafford, *with Macready in the title role, was first performed in May 1837.*

Colour lithography by Daniel Havell (1785-1826). The Bridgeman Art Library/ Stapleton Collection, UK

'mystical, strange and heavy', and it remained unperformed. *A Blot on the 'Scutcheon* did achieve three performances in 1843, but only after altercations between Browning, Forster and Macready, and not, in the end, with Macready in the cast. This marked the end of Browning's direct involvement with the theatre, and, until he effected a reconciliation some nine years later, an end to his friendship with Macready.

Paracelsus and *Strafford* interrupted Browning's work on *Sordello*, a long poem about the thirteenth-century troubadour of that name, begun probably in 1834 and published in 1840 at his father's expense (like *Paracelsus*). Here, above all, he drew on detailed historical knowledge and made few concessions, either in material or language, to the average reader of poetry; most reviewers therefore took the easy option of dismissing the poem outright. Satirical responses to the opening comment, 'Who will, may hear Sordello's story told', were legion. The reputation of Browning's poetry – fairly high after *Paracelsus* – was badly dented. Few critics took much notice of his next few volumes. He often claimed to scorn reviews, but was probably deeply wounded; in the year he died he spoke candidly to the younger writer Edmund Gosse about 'the desolateness of his early and middle life as a literary man', and how 'a blight had fallen upon his very admirers' after *Paracelsus*. Nevertheless he persevered with the same 'audacious obstinacy' which, he told Gosse, 'had made him, when a youth, determine to be a poet and nothing but a poet'.

While writing *Sordello*, in the spring of 1838, Browning made his first visit to Italy, for the convenient purpose of completing the poem 'among the scenes it describes'. Having sailed to Trieste, he spent much of his time in Venice, travelling also to such nearby places as the hill-town and ruined fortress of Asolo. On his second visit, in 1844, he landed at Naples and saw, among other places, Amalfi, Rome and Florence. Italy provided the inspiration or setting for many of his best-known poems. He was drawn to it by its importance to his predecessors, the Romantic poets Byron, Shelley and Keats, by his love of Italian Renaissance art, by the colourful and violent figures of medieval and Renaissance Italian history, and by the warmth and fertility which have so often attracted northern Europeans. Another appeal was the low cost of living in comparison with England – a practical aspect of the Brownings' romantic decision to settle in Tuscany in 1846.

Asolo provides the setting for *Pippa Passes: a Drama* (1841), in which Pippa, a young silk weaver, apparently too unimportant to have any effect on the world around her, sings as she walks, and accidentally influences her hearers' relationships and decisions. (Pippa's situation – lonely, seemingly obscure, but in fact a powerful influence – has analogies with Browning's view of his own situation after *Sordello*.) Among those who hear her are Ottima and her lover, Sebald, who have murdered Ottima's old husband. Sebald wishes the deed undone, but Ottima woos him with memories of how 'I stretched myself upon you, hands/To hands, my mouth to your hot mouth'. As she regains control of him, she tells him to bind her hair 'thrice about my brow…Crown me your queen, your spirit's arbitress,/Magnificent in sin. Say that!' But as Sebald repeats her sibilant proclamation, he is interrupted by Pippa's

Title-page of Browning's 'Sordello' (1840), an ambitious poem that was unpopular with most reviewers. In 1855, 243 copies out of the original 500 remained unsold.

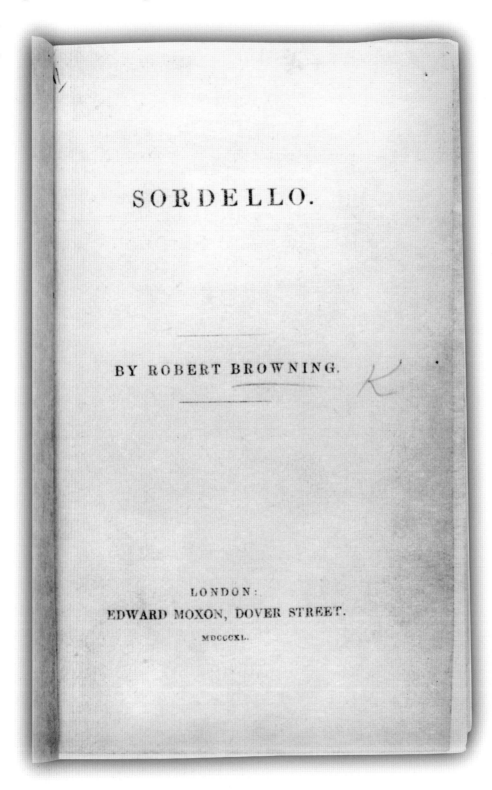

SORDELLO.

BY ROBERT BROWNING.

LONDON:
EDWARD MOXON, DOVER STREET.
MDCCCXL.

song, which concludes with the oft-quoted 'God's in his heaven -/All's right with the world!' At once he finds Ottima's beauty gone, hates her attempt to 'fascinate by sinning', and realizes fully, thanks to 'that little peasant's voice', what he has done. Pippa may at first appear to be promoting a simple, naively optimistic morality, but as the eponymous heroine passes other scenes, more questions arise. All around her are corruption and sin; all is evidently not 'right with the world', or easily righted by a song.

'My Last Duchess', in Browning's *Dramatic Lyrics* (1842), explores a no less imperfect world. The speaker is a Renaissance duke of Ferrara, talking to an envoy sent by the father of his next intended wife. The duke, as they look together at the portrait of his last duchess, is as certain of his own reasonableness as is Porphyria's lover. The duchess had

> *A heart – how shall I say? – too soon made glad,*
> *Too easily impressed; she liked whate'er*
> *She looked on, and her looks went everywhere.*
> *Sir, 'twas all one! My favour at her breast,*
> *The dropping of the daylight in the West,*
> *The bough of cherries some officious fool*
> *Broke in the orchard for her, the white mule*
> *She rode with round the terrace – all and each*
> *Would draw from her alike the approving speech,*
> *Or blush, at least. She thanked men, – good! but thanked*
> *Somehow – I know not how – as if she ranked*
> *My gift of a nine-hundred-years-old name*
> *With anybody's gift.*

It would have been too much 'stooping' for the proud duke to point out her error. Instead, 'I gave commands; then all smiles stopped together'. As a picture, she has become an object or 'piece' he can control – 'none puts by/The curtain I have drawn for you, but I' – interpret and show off as the work of the famous (fictional) painter Fra Pandolf. Only the duke can tell the picture's viewers her story, what lies behind

'The depth and passion of its earnest glance'. When he tells that story, readers and perhaps the envoy are likely to condemn the duke, not the duchess. On the other hand, as he turns to his listener at the end, it becomes apparent that the envoy and the reader have been effectively trapped, silenced, forced for a time at least to see things through the duke's eyes, forced almost into complicity with him. He ends the poem still the only speaker, still exerting his power.

In 'My Last Duchess' Browning sees truth in what he later called 'prismatic hues' – inevitably conditioned by viewpoint. This effect is enhanced by the silent presence of a listener, palpably influencing the way the speaker chooses to present himself or herself; the stated or implied presence is one of the defining features of what would later become known as 'dramatic monologue'. (The poems in *Dramatic Lyrics* are, says Browning's preface, 'for the most part Lyric in expression, always Dramatic in principle, and so many utterances of so many imaginary persons, not mine'.) Another early dramatic monologue is 'The Bishop Orders His Tomb at Saint Praxed's Church', in Browning's next collection *Dramatic Romances and Lyrics* (1845), where again the setting is Renaissance Italy. The venality and hypocrisy of the Roman Catholic church in the early sixteenth century, especially in Italy, was a commonplace, based partly in fact, partly in Protestant dogma. The dying bishop soon reveals how well he fits this tradition: he is addressing his 'Nephews – sons mine'. (Offspring of supposedly celibate clergy were sometimes passed off as nephews.) He wants to impress on them that they must build him a magnificent tomb which will outdo that of his old rival Gandolf: a tomb of basalt, jasper, lapis lazuli, surrounded by columns of 'Peach-blossom marble all', and with reliefs that blend Christian subjects with semi-naked nymphs. But the more he speaks, the more it becomes apparent that the silent 'nephews', long encouraged in their materialism by their father, will not carry out his wishes. Browning, who probably saw the church of Santa Prassede in Rome in 1844, was aware that it contains no tomb remotely like the one requested.

In 'The Bishop' Browning exposes a Renaissance prelate (and enjoys the gusto with which he sins), but he also comments on what he describes, when referring to the poem, as 'the Oxford business'. In the Oxford movement of the

237

THE TOMB AT ST. PRAXED'S.

(ROME, 15—.)

BY ROBERT BROWNING.

VANITY, saith the Preacher, vanity!
Draw round my bed: is Anselm keeping back?
Nephews — sons mine . . . ah God, I know not! Well —
She, men would have to be your mother once,
Old Gandolf envied me, so fair she was!
What's done is done, and she is dead beside,
And long ago, and I am Bishop since,
And as she died so must we die ourselves,
And thence ye may perceive the world's a dream.
Life, how and what is it? As here I lie
In this state-chamber, dying by degrees,
Hours and long hours in the dead night, I ask
"Do I live, am I dead?" Peace, peace seems all:
St. Praxed's ever was the church for peace;
And so, about this tomb of mine. I fought
With tooth and nail to save my niche, ye know:
—Old Gandolf came me in, despite my care,
For a shrewd snatch out of the corner south
To grace his carrion with, God curse the same!
Yet still my niche is not so cramp'd but thence
One sees the pulpit o' the epistle-side,
And somewhat of the choir, those silent seats,
And up into the aery dome where live
The angels, and a sunbeam's sure to lurk:
And I shall fill my slab of basalt there,
And 'neath my tabernacle take my rest
With those nine columns round me, two and two,
The odd one at my feet where Anselm stands:
Peachblossom-marble all, the rare, the ripe
As fresh-pour'd red wine of a mighty pulse
— Old Gandolf with his paltry onion-stone,
Put me where I may look at him! True peach,
Rosy and flawless: how I earn'd the prize!
Draw close: that conflagration of my church
— What then? So much was sav'd if aught were miss'd!
My sons, ye would not be my death? Go dig

Extract from Browning's 'The Bishop Orders his Tomb at Saint Praxed's Church', as first published in Hood's Magazine, *March 1845. The dying Bishop daydreams about the magnificent and distinctly secular tomb he expects to be built for him.*

The British Library
PP 5987 A

1830s and 1840s some High Church members of the Church of England outraged more orthodox Protestants by reaffirming their descent from the pre-Reformation Catholic church. In the process, they sought to increase both the splendour of church buildings and the ritual element in services. The danger of this, according to many Protestants, was a focus on beauty, on 'peach-blossom marble', rather than

God. Yet even in this poem, perhaps more evidently topical than anything Browning had written before, the controversy provides only one strand of plausible interpretation; seeing through the bishop's eyes seems to be more interesting to the poet than explicit intervention in the 'Oxford business'.

At first there seems nothing very topical about 'England in Italy' (later re-titled 'The Englishman in Italy'), also in the 1845 collection. The Englishman is trying to distract a child during autumn wind (sirocco) and rain near Sorrento. He engages her attention with colourful, dynamic word-pictures of local life – the split figs drying, the 'pink and grey jellies, your sea-fruit', the girl's brother 'all bare-legged…dancing' as he treads the grapes, the prospect of feasting

> *our grape-gleaners (two dozen,*
> *Three over one plate)*
> *With lasagne so tempting to swallow*
> *In slippery ropes,*
> *And gourds fried in great purple slices,*
> *That colour of popes.*

But there is a latent political point: amid all this fertility and abundance and apparent liberty Italians are not free. Most of the peninsula was still ruled by the reactionary king of Naples, the papacy (still more of a force to be reckoned with than Browning's jocular reference to gourds and purple robes may suggest), or the Austrian emperor and his allies.

In 1845 Browning was still living with his parents and his work was still being published at their expense. Since 1841 it had been appearing in pamphlets, which were relatively cheap to buy – *Pippa* was sixpence, *Dramatic Lyrics* one shilling and the longer *Dramatic Romances and Lyrics* two shillings – but each cost the not-insubstantial sum of £16 to produce. (Lady's maids in the service of Elizabeth Barrett earned £16 a year.) But he had written several of the poems that were to help make him famous and, in the longer term, even prosperous. He had worked in many forms, including drama, lyric, the long poem, and the dramatic monologue. *Dramatic Lyrics* and *Dramatic Romances and Lyrics* included, apart from the pieces just discussed, material ranging from a prologue of the goddess Artemis for an unwritten tragedy to the popular lyric 'Oh, to be in England,/Now that April's there…', and one of the most energetic and entertaining of children's poems, 'The Pied Piper of Hamelin', written at some speed in the spring of 1842 for Macready's son Willie.

Robert Browning, by J.C. Armytage, in Richard 'Hengist' Horne's A New Spirit of the Age, *London, 1844. Horne sent Barrett several of the original engravings, including the one for this picture; she removed it from her wall just before Browning's first visit.*

The British Library 1203 g3

≈ *Courtship*

In retrospect, Robert Browning and Elizabeth Barrett seem to have been moving towards each other long before they corresponded and met. Many of her comments on his poetry in the 1830s and early 1840s reveal the rare insight of a fellow practitioner. Writing to Mary Mitford in 1836, she wished *Paracelsus* had been clearer and more concentrated, but detected 'the pulse of poetry…a palpable power! and sudden repressed gushings of tenderness which suggest to us a depth beyond, in the affections'. In 1843, by now widely read in his work, she has, she tells Mitford, 'always held that Mr Browning was a master in clenched passion…[in] concentrated passion…burning through the metallic fissures of the language'. Miss Mitford, older than her friend, and mainly a writer of prose tales, had distinct reservations about Mr Browning's poems: 'one heap of obscurity, confusion and weakness' she called them in a letter to her friend Charles Boner in 1847. Her view of the verse was not unconnected with the personal impression she had obtained when she first saw him (coincidentally, the night before she had first met Elizabeth Barrett) at the *Ion* party in 1836. 'I remember thinking,' she told Boner, 'how exactly he resembled a boy dressed in girl's clothes…he had long ringlets and no neck-cloth' and 'seemed to be about the height and size of a boy of twelve years old.' Fortunately, she had expressed only more moderate versions of this view in her letters to Barrett. What for others was his ambition (laudable, his friends felt) was, as far as Mitford was concerned, the 'conceit of writing book upon book all bad'.

Barrett was better disposed to Browning from the beginning since she was better able to tolerate obscurity, meanings that had to be worked for, that could not be reduced to a formula or translated into prose. If you have to read *Pippa* three times, that is 'testimony both to the genius and the obscurity' she wrote to Mitford. It is worth the effort to get at the fine things in the piece; if Browning chooses thus memorably to assert his 'strong and deep individuality' in Chaldee (an ancient Mesopotamian language), 'why, he makes it worth our while to get out our dictionaries'. Mitford was forever encouraging Barrett herself to write more clearly and directly, which increased her awareness that, as writers, she and Browning both belonged to what was, for her more commonsensical friend, 'riddledom'.

In 1845, then, Browning struck up a correspondence with possibly his most appreciative reader, one who admired his work tremendously but also remained critically astute. For her part, she had always insisted that she relished informed criticism. She too found her correspondent well qualified to provide it, but few of his early responses to her work have survived. Besides the fact that he later destroyed many of his own early letters, he was a much less articulate and extensive letter-writer than she was, although in the courtship correspondence he did rise to unusual heights of communicativeness. But we know, for instance, that in May 1843 the

'I love your verses with all my heart, dear Miss Barrett...': the first and last pages of Browning's first letter to Barrett, 10 January 1845.

Wellesley College Library, Special Collections

45

poets' mutual friend John Kenyon showed Browning the manuscript of Barrett's poem 'The Dead Pan', and she was delighted when Kenyon showed her Browning's note praising its 'famous versification'.

It was Kenyon who put the poets in contact. He had tried to arrange for Browning to call on Barrett in 1842, but she had avoided this visit, as she avoided most visits, on the grounds of ill health. Then, in 1844, while Browning was still in Italy, Kenyon gave Browning's sister, Sarianna, a copy of Barrett's new *Poems*. Some time in the first few days of 1845 her brother, reading the book, came upon the flattering reference to his poetry in 'Lady Geraldine's Courtship'. With Kenyon's encouragement, he wrote to her on 10 January to express his appreciation of her work: he liked the 'fresh strange music, the affluent language, the exquisite pathos and true new brave thought'. It was the same kind of praise – slightly vague but evidently deeply felt – that she had bestowed on him. With characteristic enthusiasm, he went on to declare, famously, 'I do, as I say, love these Books with all my heart – and I love you too.' Obviously she did not take this statement, in a first letter, quite literally. What Browning meant at the time becomes clearer in the light of the way he contrasted their approach to poetry in his next letter (13 January): 'You speak out, you, – I only make men and women speak – give you truth broken into prismatic hues, and fear the pure white light, even if it is in me.' In other words, he was convinced that her poetry accurately expressed her, in a sense was her. This was among the reasons why she delayed meeting him for the next four months: she feared that a pale, secluded, at least partly invalid woman in her late thirties could not live up to the image Browning derived from the poems. (She had deftly managed to avoid meeting several other correspondents who had sought the favour of an interview.) Browning had the opposite problem. Since he had not, he felt, laid himself bare in his poems – had not, as he told her, written 'R.B., a poem' – he needed physically to meet her if she was to understand him completely. His great social confidence would then either charm or repel her.

In the meantime, however, the correspondence was fuelled by each poet's eager desire for expert opinions on their reading and writing. (No longer needing Mitford to fulfil this function, Barrett began to write to her less frequently.) They wrote about their families and work, English and French novelists, Greek literature and Italy. She told him in March about her ideas for a modern, controversial 'sort of novel-poem' – *Aurora Leigh* eventually – and he began sending her, act by act, his play *Luria* and, more importantly, the poems of *Dramatic Lyrics and Romances*. Her comments, most of which Browning acted on, were detailed and practical – suggestions for an apter word, a clearer title. Literature, particularly at the beginning, provided a safe meeting-point, a way of developing a personal relationship while they were apparently engaged in professional discussion.

The correspondence proved so fulfilling on both parts that Browning succeeded in persuading Barrett, nervous though she was about the prospect, to let him visit her. On 20 May 1845, at 3.00 in the afternoon, he at last ascended the stairs to her third-floor room at the back of 50 Wimpole Street. In person they not only lived up to each other's expectations, but exceeded them: she found him better-looking than portraits suggested, and he soon discovered that she was not, as he had been led to believe, disabled by a serious spine injury. It was some time, however, before he could persuade her that he was sincerely in love with her. One reason for this was her perception, expressed in a letter to Browning in December 1845, that most marriages were unhappy, often because of male vanity and disloyalty. She was irritated by the assumptions about male superiority entertained by, among others, the Rev. George Hunter, whom she had first known in Sidmouth and later in London,

50 Wimpole Street, Barrett's home in 1838 and 1841-46. The building was demolished in 1912.

Photograph c. 1900, Westminster City Archives

and who seems to have been her disappointed suitor. Later she was by turns bored and annoyed by the opinionated James Bevan, the man who was about to marry her cousin Arabella Hedley. But Barrett was well aware from an early stage that Browning did not share conventional male attitudes to matrimony, did not expect to exercise authority over a wife; his own parents' marriage was evidently built on mutual respect. In better health than she had been for years, Barrett was beginning to see the future more positively and the past less so. By 20 March she was already telling him how, in her illness after Bro's death, she came to realize how much of life she had missed. Confined to one room and, she thought, about to die, she *turned to thinking, with some bitterness…that I had stood blind in this temple I was about to leave – that I had seen no Human nature, that my brothers and sisters of the earth were names to me, that I had beheld no great mountain or river, nothing in fact. I was as a man dying who had not read Shakespeare, and it was too late!*

If she could not escape from her seclusion, she felt, she would be effectively 'a *blind poet*'.

With hindsight Browning, experienced in at least some aspects of the external world she now longed for, arrived on cue. In fact he nearly arrived too fast, nearly throwing the relationship away when, impetuously, he wrote, after his first visit, the only one of the courtship letters which has not survived. This contained, we know from the reply, a strong declaration of love, perhaps a marriage proposal. Barrett answered that she could not see him again if he ever repeated such overtures, but made it clear that, with that condition, she was eager to continue the relationship. Browning then saved the day by writing a long letter in which he apologized, but at the same time succeeded in suggesting that she had misunderstood his intentions. She accepted this and, at his request, sent back the declaration for him to destroy. The correspondence and the conversations, sticking at first to such safe subjects as poetry, were able to continue.

That Barrett let the visits continue shows how far her resistance to personal contact with the world outside Wimpole Street was giving way. That she had allowed Browning to visit at all was, in view of how much she feared her father's reaction, courageous. Edward Barrett had always expected absolute obedience from his family. He wanted to be briefed about their movements and their friendships. Even apparently innocuous activities were frowned upon; for instance, in July 1845 he would almost certainly have forbidden his son Alfred and several other Barretts to go to the country for a picnic in Mary Mitford's garden at Three Mile Cross had they not, with some help from Elizabeth, managed to keep him in ignorance about the trip. And it became steadily clearer that he would not tolerate the marriage of any of his children, even once they were many years older than he had been at the time of his own marriage. The fierceness of his views became apparent some years before

Elizabeth Barrett Browning and Robert Browning

'The Lost Mistress',
Byam Shaw's illustration
for Browning's poem
beginning 'All's over,
then: does truth sound
bitter/As one at first
believes?' The poem may
have been written at, or
soon after, the time when
Barrett rejected his first,
premature declaration of
love in May 1845.

The British Library
556* a3/3

50

Barrett met Browning, when her sister Henrietta had asked permission to go somewhere with a young man, or possibly to receive him as a suitor. Barrett told Browning how, on her father's refusal,

> *at a word she gave up all – at a word…A child never submitted more meekly*
> *to a revoked holiday. Yet how she was made to suffer – Oh, the dreadful scenes!*
> *– and only because she had seemed to feel a little…I hear how her knees were*
> *made to ring upon the floor, now! – she was carried out of the room in strong*
> *hysterics…Though I was quite well at that time and suffered only by sympathy,*
> *I fell down flat upon my face in a fainting-fit. Arabel thought I was dead.*

William Surtees Cook, later a suitor of Henrietta's, was allowed to visit quite freely, but only because he was related to the family. If her father had known about Cook's designs on Henrietta, he would at once have denied him access to the house.

Browning visited Wimpole Street ninety-one times, usually starting at 3 p.m. and ending first at 4.30, then later up to 5 or 6 p.m. Barrett chose this time of day in order to draw as little attention as possible to the visits. Her brothers were often out in the afternoon, and her father normally came home from business at 7 p.m. Barrett's maid, Elizabeth Wilson (1817–1902), helped arrangements to run as smoothly as possible, sometimes even deflecting other visitors. Henrietta and Arabel Barrett met Browning, but he did not encounter her brothers (except George, elsewhere in London, as an acquaintance) and never met her father. Edward Barrett knew that Browning – the 'pomegranate poet' he once sarcastically called him for his *Bells and Pomegranates* – came to see his daughter, but had no idea how often and little or no suspicion of how the relationship was developing. Once, late in the courtship period, when he arrived home, he was displeased to hear that Browning was still on the premises: 'Well, it appears, Ba, that *that man* has spent the whole day with you,' he observed later.

In late August 1845, when Browning had risked and Barrett had accepted a second declaration of love, he several times suggested that he should, straightforwardly and honourably, go to Edward Barrett and explain how matters stood. But Elizabeth Barrett refused to let him do anything of the kind, fearing confrontation and her own collapse under the strain of it, and knowing how implacable were her father's views on marriage and parental authority – or, as she more delicately put it to Browning, his 'obliquity' or 'eccentricity – or something beyond – on one class of subjects'.

Barrett must have wrestled with her feelings about her father, so long the dominant figure in her life, even more than she told Browning. She looked back to the time when, after her return from Torquay, she and her father had seemed, in their grief for Bro, to recover their old closeness. In the evenings, for years, they prayed together, hand in hand, alone in her room. She tried to explain to Browning what biographers are still trying to explain – how Edward Barrett could be so unreasonable. In the very letter of January 1846 where she talks of his coldness and isolation and of being 'made to suffer in the suffering of those by my side…depressed by petty daily sadnesses and terrors', she also refers twice to his 'high qualities', his 'courage and fortitude', uprightness and honour and declares – by this time Browning might have begged leave to doubt it – 'you would esteem him, you would like him, I think'.

There are various ways of trying to account for Mr Barrett's attitudes. He cannot easily be diagnosed and dismissed as the ogre of Rudolf Besier's play *The Barretts of Wimpole Street* (1930), consumed with incestuous passion for his daughter. He hated, as did his daughter, the idea of the family breaking up, and, like her, was uneasy with strangers. He had what seemed to her 'a miserable misconception of the limits and character of parental rights'. He had a notion of her angelic purity, and his ideal of her was no doubt sullied when she married. Recently one writer on the Brownings, Julia Markus, has raised the possibility that he feared there might be black, slave blood among his forebears, and that this is why he was desperate that none of his children should reproduce. But no single theory seems completely convincing. Edward Moulton-Barrett should have been a figure in a Browning monologue: fixated yet, like Browning's creations, complex, not quite reducible to his fixation, not fully explicable.

What finally enabled the once-dependent daughter to break away seems to have been her father's reaction to the idea of her going abroad for the winter for the good of her health. Her doctor encouraged her to go to Italy, perhaps Pisa. In

September 1845 she put the scheme to her father. According to her he gave his permission, but in 'a hard, cold letter'. (His relationships, and his posthumous reputation, were not helped by the way in which, apparently on principle, he refused to explain his decisions or, in this case, why his agreement was so grudging.) Questioned further, he said he 'washed his hands of me altogether'. Elizabeth Barrett therefore gave up the Pisa idea, in part because of her father's likely fury with George and Arabel, who had also been involved in the planning. Alienated more completely than before, Barrett decided that 'I had believed Papa to have loved me more than he obviously does'.

Barrett promised that she would marry Browning at the end of the summer of 1846, provided she were well enough. She was increasingly active in 1845–46, coming downstairs, walking more, even visiting Regent's Park, Westminster Abbey and Kew Gardens, where she surreptitiously picked a pansy to send to Browning. But she sought to delay the marriage, and her father's inevitable reaction, as long as possible. On the same logic, she avoided as far as possible telling her siblings and friends that she was going to get married. John Kenyon, for instance, was kept in ignorance so that he could not be blamed for failing to denounce them to the patriarch, though both poets sometimes thought he suspected something. Browning even had difficulty in persuading her that he could tell his parents.

Whatever her father's reaction to her marriage, Barrett was confident that she and her husband could survive financially: her paternal grandmother had left her the very considerable sum of £4000 in 1829, and her uncle, Samuel Barrett, had left her money and shares in a merchant ship, the *David Lyon*, in 1840. In August 1846 she had £8000 in government stocks, yielding an annual income of about £170. Income from the ship was more variable and was immediately reinvested, but totalled up to £200 a year. And there was also the likelihood of some earnings from poetry.

Browning, who had little prospect of poetry sales and no income, felt sensitive about the imbalance in their positions. He rightly suspected that some members of Barrett's family would say he had married her for her money, and thought of finding paid employment, perhaps in the diplomatic service. But no job appeared and Barrett counselled him to stick to his craft. He salved his conscience by borrowing £100 from his father and later by having their friend Kenyon draw up a marriage settlement which stipulated that, in the event of her death, her goods and money would go not to her husband – otherwise, the automatic legal inheritor – but to her children or, if there were none, her sisters.

What finally triggered events was her father's arbitrary announcement, in September 1846, that the family would soon move to the country while 50 Wimpole Street was redecorated. Encouraged now by Barrett to act decisively for both of them, Browning declared that 'We must be *married directly*.' He was no longer prepared to wait, no longer to endure the stress-related headaches of the last difficult months. They had been making detailed plans to travel to Pisa for some time, but her maid, Wilson, who had agreed to accompany them, had to do much of the actual organising. She and the groom's cousin, James Silverthorne, were witnesses to the marriage, at 11.00 a.m. on 12 September in St Marylebone Church. They then went back to their family homes, with much still to prepare and with difficult letters for Barrett to write to her father and others explaining her departure. On the afternoon of 19 September Barrett, with Wilson and Flush, walked, and then, having nearly fainted, took a cab to meet Browning at Hodgson's bookshop in Great Marylebone Street. They travelled by train to Southampton, by boat to Le Havre, and on by coach to Rouen and Paris.

From Paris they intended to proceed as rapidly as possible to Pisa. Fortunately, however, Browning sent a note to their mutual friend Anna Jameson, who was staying in Paris, inviting her, to her initial mystification and continuing astonishment, to 'come and see your friend and my wife EBB'. Jameson found Elizabeth Barrett Browning, as she wrote to her friend Lady Byron, the poet's estranged wife and widow, 'nervous, frightened, ashamed, agitated, happy, miserable' and very exhausted, and Browning anxious and impractical. She decided that she must take charge of them. She moved the couple into her hotel, persuaded Barrett Browning that she must recuperate in Paris for a week, and agreed that she and her niece would accompany them on the rest of the journey. After this the journey was less worrying, although at Orléans Barrett had to face the trial of opening the letter (no longer extant) in which, as feared, her father cast her off, refusing from then on to see her or answer her letters. Jameson wrote to Lady Byron from Avignon that 'not only we have had to carry her fainting from the carriage but from her extreme thinness and weakness, every few hours' journey has bruised her all over'. But she was impressed by the new wife's courage and patience, the husband's joyous 'poetical fancies and antics' and tenderness, and their 'mutual deportment...marked by the most graceful propriety'. When they reached Pisa, Jameson was still concerned that, for all his charm, Browning was 'in all the common things of this life the most impractical of men', but twelve days later she was able to report that they had found comfortable accommodation and 'all their arrangements are as sensible as if they had never spoken anything but prose in their lives and they are so happy!'

Lifecast of the Brownings' hands by their friend Harriet Hosmer, 1853.

National Portrait Gallery, London

❧ *Marriage*

Elizabeth Barrett Browning nourished hopes, right up to her father's death in 1857, that he would relent and forgive her. When she visited London in 1851, good relations with her brothers were largely restored (her sisters had never wavered in their support for her), but on making overtures to her father she received a 'violent and unsparing' reply, together with all the letters she had sent him from Italy – unopened. 'If I had committed murder and forgery,' she wrote to Henrietta, 'I don't see how Papa could have shown his sense of it otherwise than he has done.' In spite of this unhealed wound, she succeeded in entering positively, after 1846, into a new life of marriage, extensive friendships, and passionate involvement in Italian politics. Under these varied influences she produced work of a new range and quality. For the first few years in particular, her health, though never robust, greatly improved; indeed Anna Jameson claimed, just before she left Pisa in early November 1846, that she wasn't '*improved*, but *transformed* rather'.

Robert Browning was happy, too, although he missed his parents, worrying especially about his elderly mother, and for the first three years in Italy found himself writing almost no new poetry, although he revised earlier work for the *Poems* he published in 1849. 'Being too happy doesn't agree with literary activity as well as I should have thought,' his wife noted. Her main work in Pisa during the rest of the autumn was on 'The Runaway Slave at Pilgrim's Point', begun at the end of 1845 and eventually published in the Boston anti-slavery compilation *The Liberty Bell* in 1848. In Pisa the Brownings lived in an apartment in the Collegio di Ferdinando, near the cathedral and Leaning Tower. Even after they discovered that they were being overcharged, everything seemed wonderfully cheap. In March 1847 Barrett Browning had a miscarriage after five months of pregnancy (undetected until near the end) but, to judge from her letters, remained surprisingly little depressed. She was evidently determined, after the momentous step she had taken in marrying at all, to stay positive. She miscarried again a year later, this time after two months.

In theory it was exciting to be living in Pisa, the destination so often talked and read about in Wimpole Street. But in fact it soon became rather dull. There was comparatively little social life and the new bride was, besides, mostly confined to the

We were black, we were black!

We had no claim to love & bliss

So what marvel if each turned to each?

They wrung my cold hands out of his —

They dragged him ... why, I crawled to touch

... in the dust .. not much,

Ye Pilgrim-souls, though plain as this!

I am black, I am black —

I wore a child upon my breast..

An amulet that hang too black,

And in my unrest could not rest —

And thus we sat moaning, we child & mother,

One to another, one to another

Until all ended for the best.

So hark! I will tell you low ... low ..

I am black you see —

And the babe that lay on my bosom so,

Was far too white .. too white for me;

As white as the ladies who scorned to pray

Beside me at church but yesterday,

Though my tears had washed a place for my knee

*Stanzas from Barrett's
'The Runaway Slave at
Pilgrim's Point'.
A black slave describes
how she was separated
from the man she loved
and then raped by her
white masters. She lives
in a world where 'We
were black, we were
black!/We had no claim
to love and bliss...'.*

*The British Library
Ashley MS A2517 f5*

Collegio, apart from short walks, by her anxious husband. Barrett Browning in particular felt starved of good books. She was an insatiable reader of novels, especially contemporary French novels, and few of these were to be had in Pisa, while both she and Browning found recent Italian novels unexpectedly uninspiring. Soon after her recovery from the first miscarriage, in the spring of 1847, they moved the fifty or so miles to the larger, livelier and more strikingly beautiful Florence. Barrett Browning later described to Mitford this city set

> *in its garden-ground of vineyards and olive-trees, sung round by the nightingales day and night, nay, sung* into *by the nightingales, for as you walk along the streets in the evening the song trickles down into them till they stop to listen.*

A place for poets, Mitford might have reflected. But her friend goes on, a little more practically, to sum Florence up as 'cheap, tranquil, cheerful, beautiful, within the limit of civilization yet out of the crush of it'.

It was in June 1847, after three months in rooms in Via delle Belle Donne, that the Brownings rented seven furnished rooms on the first floor of Casa Guidi, near the Pitti Palace. In October, after difficulties in renewing the lease, they moved again and ended up in more expensive accommodation, but in May 1848 they were able to return to Casa Guidi, this time taking the rooms unfurnished. This remained their home for the next thirteen years. In 1861 the American writer and journalist Kate Field recalled the large drawing-room full of paintings, tapestries, easy chairs, sofas, tables and overflowing carved bookcases. Here Barrett Browning would sit in a low armchair by the door, beside 'a small table, strewn with writing-materials, books and newspapers'. (Browning's 'retreat' was 'the long room filled with plaster casts' and drawings.)

It was from the front windows of Casa Guidi on 12 September 1847 – their first wedding anniversary – that the Brownings witnessed the celebrations when Grand Duke Leopoldo II of Tuscany, the Austrian-supported local ruler, granted the citizens of Florence the right to form their own civic guard. This in itself was a small step, but seemed important at a time when monarchs all over Italy were being forced

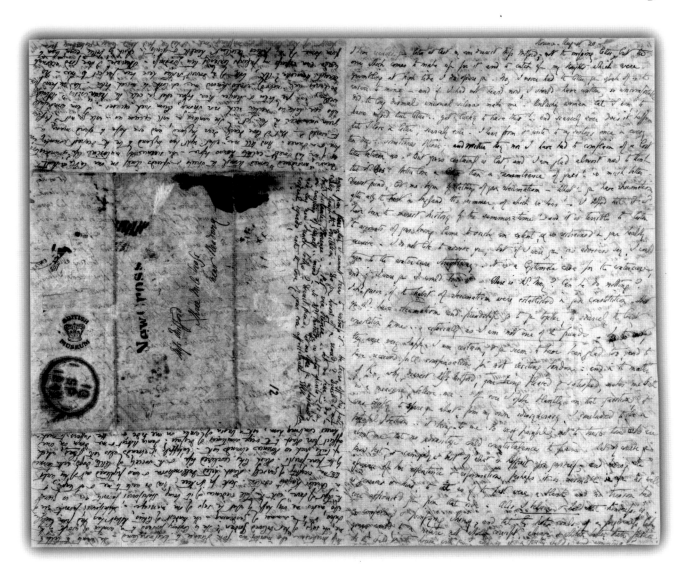

to grant concessions to their people. Barrett Browning's response was to write a poem called 'A Meditation in Tuscany', which later became Part One of *Casa Guidi Windows* (1851). At the beginning of this poem, as a small boy sings about Liberty the Beautiful and a grateful procession nears the palace, Italy seems at last to be taking vigorous action to make up for centuries of living as 'impassioned nympholept' – idealist lover – of 'her own past'. Modern Florentines will at last act like their noble forebears, the artists and poets – Dante, Petrarch, Giotto, Michelangelo.

Previous pages:

'This Florence is unspeakably beautiful, by grace both of nature and art', Barrett told Mary Russell Mitford in her letter of 20 August 1847. Painting of Florence from Ponte Vecchio by Giovanni Signorini.

The Bridgeman Art Library/Gavin Graham Gallery, London

122 15

Of other mens achievements (who achieved
By loving art beyond the master), he
Was old Margheritone and conceived
Never at youngest & most ecstasy
A Virgin like that smile of one, that heaved
The death sigh from his heart. If certainly
Margheritone sickened at the smell
Of Cimabue's laurel, " Let him go!" –
Strong Cimabue stood up very well
In spite of Giotto's = and Angelico
The artist-saint kept smiling in his cell
The smile with which he welcomed in the slow
Inbreak of angels, (whitening through the dim
That he should paint them) when the sudden sense
Of Raffael's future was revealed to him
By force of his own fair works' competence.
The same blue waters where the dolphins swim
Suggest the tritons – through the blue Immense
Strike out, all swimmers! cling not in the way
Of one another, so to sink; but learn
The strong man's impulse, catch the freshening spray
He throws up in his motions, and discern
By his calm westering eye, the time of day!
O God, thou hast set us noble gifts to earn
Beside thy Heaven & thee! and when I say

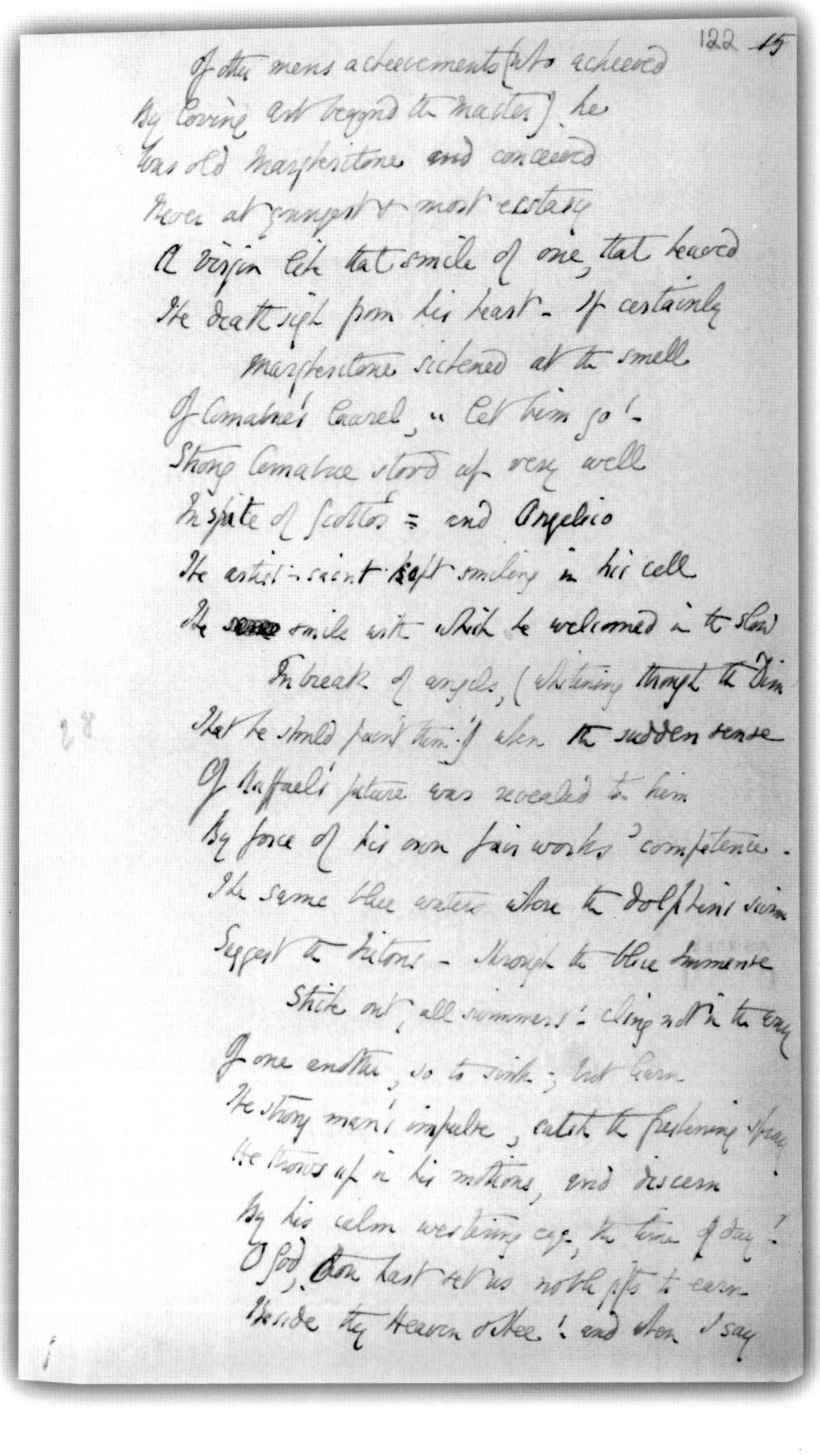

Right:

A passage from Barrett's Casa Guidi Windows, Part One, *where she encourages modern Italians to live up to the achievements of their predecessors, not to cling to the past; the old Florentine painters themselves looked to the future, Cimabue smiling on the work of his successor Giotto, Fra Angelico anticipating the genius of Raphael.*

TheBritish Library Ashley MS A224 f122

In the spring of 1848 she sent 'A Meditation in Tuscany' to *Blackwood's Edinburgh Magazine*. William Blackwood, the publisher, finally replied seven months later, calling the work 'grand' but beyond human comprehension and in need of explanatory notes. The details of events in Tuscany were little known to most readers, but probably a political poem by a male author of similar status would have been given a more favourable reception. Eventually, her poem was published in 1851 by Chapman & Hall, the publishers of virtually all the Brownings' works between 1849 and the mid-1860s. By the time the poem appeared, the political situation had changed drastically. The Florentines had proclaimed a republic, but the Grand Duke had been restored to power with the aid of Austrian troops. Barrett Browning watched, again from Casa Guidi, as the Austrians arrived on 5 May 1849, received in silence by the Florentines. She described the scene in *Casa Guidi Windows Part Two*:

> *The regular tramp of horse and tread of men*
> *Did smite the silence like an anvil black*
> *And sparkless.*
>
> *…Horse, foot, artillery, cannons rolling on,*
> *Like blind slow storm-clouds gestant with the heat*
> *Of undeveloped lightnings, each bestrode*
> *By a single man, dust white from head to heel,*
> *Indifferent as the dreadful thing he rode.*

This second part of the poem laments that the song with which Part One began was apparently only a child's song, taken up for a moment with 'unintentioned voice' before the child breaks off and goes back to sleep on its mother's lap. With reference to the treacherous Grand Duke, she asks patriots to absolve her of 'my woman's fault,/That ever I believed the man was true'. (Contemporaries usually took this, of course, as an admission of female weakness, but it also suggests how rarely men are 'true'.) She criticizes the Tuscans' failure to match words with deeds, liberty songs with an understanding of 'the serious, sacred meaning and full use/Of freedom for a nation', but also wants to know why richer nations, who in 1851 were showing off their wares in London at the Great Exhibition in 'the gorgeous Crystal Palace', had nothing to give 'poor Italia'. Britain was not the only culprit, readers at home must have been relieved to hear: Austria tyrannized Italy, Russia the Poles, America its slaves, and France intervened to end the 1848/9 republic in Rome. 'Alas, great nations have great shames, I say.'

Finally Barrett Browning makes clear her refusal to give up hope for Italy: the future, she rightly believes, lies with the kingdom of Piedmont-Savoy, the only part of the country which stood free of the Austrian, papal and Bourbon bloc; and perhaps the good omen of the singing child will not, after all, prove wrong. She concludes the work with a hopeful vision of 'my own young Florentine,/Not two years old', standing in the sun which floods through Casa Guidi windows.

The 'young Florentine' was born Robert Wiedemann Barrett Browning on 9 March 1849, three days after his mother's forty-third birthday. The baby was known as 'Wiedemann' – his paternal grandmother's maiden name – but soon after he could speak, his usual name became 'Penini' and later 'Pen'. His father thought that this resulted from the child's unsuccessful attempt to pronounce his more formal name, while Pen himself believed it came from 'trying to pronounce 'Nini' – the name Italians give their children'. The new parents, immensely relieved that the pregnancy had come to term and that mother and child were both pronounced healthy, were briefly in festive mood. But less than ten days later Browning's mother, Sarah Anna, died after a heart-attack. She never knew of her grandson's birth. The blow was the more terrible, as other family members were aware, because Browning had not seen her for two and a half years and had never before suffered bereavement (unlike his wife), and because of the cruel contrast with the joy at Pen's birth. For months he seemed inconsolable. He slowly began to recover from his grief, trying to distract himself by walking and riding in the woods and hills as much as possible during a summer spent at Bagni di Lucca.

It was here that Barrett Browning at last showed him the sequence of love sonnets she had written, unknown to him, during their courtship. He was, of course, personally moved by such poems as 'How do I love thee...', but also convinced her that she must publish these *Sonnets from the Portuguese*. ('The Portuguese' is partly intended to refer to Catarina, the woman in love with the sixteenth-century

*Manuscript of sonnet 43
'How do I love thee?' in
Barrett Browning's*
Sonnets from the
Portuguese.

*The British Library
Add. MS 43487 f49*

XLIII

How do I love thee? Let me count the ways!
I love thee to the depth & breadth & height
My soul can reach, when feeling out of sight
For the ends of Being and Ideal Grace.
I love thee to the level of everyday's
Most quiet need, by sun & candlelight —
I love thee freely, as men strive for Right; —
I love thee purely, as they turn from Praise!.
I love thee with the passion put to use
In my old griefs ;; and with my childhood's faith.
I love thee with the love I seemed to lose
With my lost Saints! — I love thee with the breath
Smiles, tears, of all my life — and, if God choose,
I shall but love thee better after death.

Portuguese poet Camoens in Barrett Browning's earlier poem 'Catarina to Camoens'. The title also, modestly if not over seriously, implies that the sonnets are translated from Portuguese originals.) The sonnets are the only part of her work which has rarely, if ever, been out of fashion; during the twentieth century they went through more than a hundred editions (often aimed at lovers and produced in decorative formats). This sort of popularity has perhaps somewhat blunted the original inventiveness of the poems and their challenge to the almost uniformly male tradition of sonnet-writing.

Browning was still, in his mourning as in the happiness that preceded it, writing no poetry. Soon after arriving in Bagni di Lucca in early July, he wrote to his sister that for three months he had been thinking only of their mother and 'catching at any little fancy of finding something which it would have pleased her I should do'. Possibly it was this thought that at last enabled him to begin writing again, since his devout mother would have been glad that the poem he began back in Florence in November – *Christmas-Eve and Easter-Day* – was on a religious subject.

The poem sold 200 copies soon after its appearance in April 1850, but sales then trailed off; Chapman & Hall still had copies available in 1864. Religion was not in itself necessarily bad for sales – the huge bestseller of 1850 was Tennyson's *In Memoriam* – but Browning's approach to the subject was characteristically intelligent and oblique, his own views difficult to pin down, whereas Tennyson's meditations, his periods of doubt and belief, were centred clearly on the personal experience of loss. Reviews of Browning's poem were generally favourable but few in number; his reputation had still not fully recovered from *Sordello*, and he was in danger now of becoming typecast as his wife's husband, a minor poet appended to a major one. Ironically, this would later be precisely *her* reputation. Chapman & Hall had taken on Browning almost as part of a 'job lot' with the more saleable Barrett Browning. Her *Poems*, published in November 1850, including *Sonnets from the Portuguese* as well as earlier poems, many of them extensively revised, attracted much interest. Even before this, there were suggestions, among them one in the June edition of *The Athenaeum*, that she was the most suitable candidate to succeed Wordsworth as poet laureate – a striking proposition in the male-dominated establishment of the period. In the event, Tennyson was appointed.

From all that those who only heard it,
In their simplicity thought and averred it,
Had yet a meaning quite as respectable:
For, among other doctrines delectable,
Was he not surely the first to insist on,
The natural sovereignty of our race? —
Here the lecturer came to a pausing-place.
And while his cough, like a drouthy piston,
Tried to dislodge the husk that grew to him,
I siezed the occasion of bidding adieu to him,
The Vesture still within my hand.

16.

I could interpret its command.
This time He would not bid me enter
The exhausted airbell of the Critic.   /air-bell
Truth's atmosphere may grow mephitic
When Papist struggles with Dissenter,
Impregnating its pristine clarity,
— One, by his daily fare's vulgarity,
Its gust of broken meat and garlic;
— One, by his soul's too-much presuming,
To turn the frankincense's fuming
And vapours of the candle starlike
Into the cloud her wings she buoys on:
And each that sets the purulent air thing,
Poisoning it for healthy breathing —
But the Critic leaves no air to poison;
Pumps out by a ruthless ingenuity
Atom by atom, and leaves you vacuity.
Thus much of Christ, does he reject?
And what, retain? His intellect?
What is it I must reverence duly?
Poor intellect for worship, truly,
Which tells me simply what was told
(If mere morality, bereft
Of the God in Christ, be all that's left)
Elsewhere by voices manifold;
With this advantage, that the state important
Made no wise ~~~~~~~~~~~~ the stumble

Extract from the manuscript of Browning's long religious poem 'Christmas Eve and Easter Day' (1850), with Barrett's additions and corrections.

Victoria & Albert Museum, London

The drawing-room at Casa Guidi, the Brownings' home in Florence. Barrett Browning wrote in this room, which, like the rest of the apartment, has recently been restored and is open to the public between April and November.

Goeway Collection, F.W. Olin Library, Mills College, California

In Florence the Brownings were visited by many people, mainly English and American, who recorded their impressions of their hosts. They were usually struck by the cordiality of their welcome and the contrast between husband and wife: Browning playing the piano exuberantly or advancing, hand outstretched, to greet the guests, Barrett Browning sitting quietly to receive them. Many found it easy to respond to what Bayard Taylor, an American travel writer and poet, called Browning's 'lively, cheerful manner, quick voice, and perfect self-possession'. The novelist Nathaniel Hawthorne, invited to a gathering in the drawing-room at Casa Guidi, found him 'very efficient in keeping up conversation with everybody'; he 'seemed to be in all parts of the room and in every group at the same moment; a most vivid and quick-thoughted person – logical and common-sensible, as, I presume, poets generally are in their daily talk'. Hawthorne was 'rather surprised', like many people who met Browning later, that 'his conversation should be so clear, and so much to the purpose at the moment, since his poetry can seldom proceed far without running into the high grass of latent meanings and obscure allusions'. Meeting him again a few weeks later, Hawthorne was delighted by Browning's 'nonsense', which, he acutely observed, was 'the true bubble and effervescence of a bright and powerful mind'; 'I should like him much,' he added more wistfully, 'and should make him like me, if opportunities were favourable.'

Hawthorne felt drawn to Barrett Browning too, but, like others who met her briefly, was a little mystified. Visitors often found her 'ethereal', but Hawthorne the novelist could not resist developing further the idea of her (and Pen's) slightness and other-worldliness:

> *a pale, small person, scarcely embodied at all; at any rate, only substantial enough to put forth her slender fingers to be grasped, and to speak with a shrill, yet sweet, tenuity of voice. Really, I do not see how Mr Browning can suppose that he has an earthly wife any more than an earthly child; both are of the elfin-race, and will flit away from him some day when he least thinks of it.*

Anne Thackeray, daughter of the novelist William Makepeace Thackeray, knew Barrett Browning more intimately and found her more congenial. Thackeray was sixteen when she first encountered the poet's 'motherly advance', in which, she says in her memoirs, 'there was something more than kindness…there was an implied interest, equality, and understanding which is very difficult to describe and impossible to forget'. After they first met she wrote in her diary 'I think Mrs Browning is the greatest woman I ever saw in all my life. She is very small, she is brown, with dark eyes and dead brown hair; she has white teeth, and a low, curious voice;…she rarely laughs, but is always cheerful and smiling; her eyes are very bright'.

But she was not always quite as calm as the memoir-writers tend to report. In December 1852 she told Ellen Twisleton, young American wife of an English politician, that 'it was hard for her to be always [away] from her family, for she was of an anxious disposition and always building "dungeons in the air"', and, as this slightly self-mocking remark suggests, she was not as humourless as some people thought; 'none possessed a quicker sense of the grotesque, or more keenly relished an absurdity than did she' according to the American sculptor Hatty Hosmer. Hosmer cites her friend's helpless laughter when Browning, with the aid of some boards and ropes, and with desperate prayers and imprecations in several languages, re-enacted a downhill ride in a runaway donkey cart. On another occasion Barrett Browning, Hosmer and another American friend, Elizabeth Clementine Kinney, decided to disguise themselves as young men in order to see some paintings in a monastery which prohibited access to women. They were to pass themselves off as students, with Kinney's husband and Browning as their teachers. At Casa Guidi, amid much hilarity, the three women put on their costumes. Kinney was delighted to see Barrett Browning bright-eyed with glee and looking younger than usual with her heavy curls concealed under a wig. But in this case the laughter soon ended in tears: Barrett Browning's enthusiasm, as Kinney soon realized, had been at least partly opium-induced, and she wandered euphorically into the street before the others noticed. Here, in her probably not altogether convincing disguise, she began to attract a crowd of bemused onlookers. Suddenly she began to cry, expecting any moment to be arrested, and to avoid further scandal Browning insisted that the whole scheme be abandoned.

In June 1851 the Brownings left Italy for an extended stay in France and England, returning to Florence the following November. In Paris they became friends with Joseph Milsand, a French critic with an unusual degree of insight into Browning's work – credited, indeed, with having coined the term 'dramatic monologue'. In later years he became perhaps Browning's closest friend. The great event in Paris during the Brownings' stay was Louis Napoleon Bonaparte's *coup d'état* of December 1851. A year later he proclaimed himself Emperor Napoleon III. In spite of her generally liberal views, Elizabeth Barrett Browning soon became an ardent supporter of Louis Napoleon, chiefly because she hoped that he would, as he promised, intervene decisively in Italian affairs on the side of Piedmont and independence. (In the long term, her hopes turned out to be at least partly justified.) Robert Browning was more sceptical, rightly judging the French ruler to be more politician than idealist. In Paris his wife also met one of her earlier idols, George Sand. Again Browning was unimpressed, disapproving particularly of Sand's cold manner and the sycophantic and clearly unrespectable males who surrounded her. But both Brownings enjoyed the liveliness of Paris, and on the whole agreed to differ on these matters.

In London, where they spent the summer and early autumn of 1851, Barrett Browning renewed contact with family members, including Henrietta, who had now finally married Surtees Cook and been disinherited, and Arabel. As always, conciliatory approaches to their father failed. An active social life, however, helped provide distraction from this sad state of affairs: the Brownings saw Kenyon, Forster, Jameson, Carlyle, Horne and many others, several of them, like Horne, meeting for the first time their former correspondent, the then-secluded Miss Barrett. She also now, at last, met Browning's father and sister. When they in turn came to Paris later in the year, the elder Robert Browning confessed rather sheepishly to his son that he was having problems with a widow, Minny von Müller. Although he did not reveal all the details at this stage, it later became apparent that he had impulsively proposed marriage to her only to change his mind and accuse her, mistakenly, of intended bigamy. To his family as well as himself the affair became highly embarrassing. In court, in July 1852, the unfortunate widower was defended as 'a poor old dotard in love', but had £800 in damages awarded against him for breach of promise and defamation. Unable to pay, he took the option of fleeing to Paris, where he spent the last fourteen years of his life patiently looked after by his daughter Sarianna and happily absorbed in his studies and the bookstalls.

To Henriette Corkran, young daughter of an American correspondent in Paris who came to know the family, Browning's 'retiring, shy old father [the von Müller affair was evidently an aberration], with his quaint ways, simplicity and unworldliness' seemed 'much more like a man of genius than his celebrated son'. The son, when he visited the Corkrans, had turned out to be an unpoetically 'cheerful gentleman in a brown overcoat' who ate 'with avidity' a quantity of bread and butter 'and big slices of plum-cake...never uttered a word that in any way suggested a poetical thought' and had well-brushed hair.

≈ *Men and Women*

Browning may not have lived up to the child's idea of a poet, but in the early 1850s he began to produce some of his most interesting poems. Most of the pieces in *Men and Women* (1855) were written in Florence, Bagni di Lucca and Rome between the beginning of 1853 and the autumn of 1854. This newly fecund period began with a New Year's resolution, which he kept, or nearly kept for a few days at least, to write a poem every day. Barrett Browning, although troubled with racking coughs – her health was never again to be as good as during the first years of marriage – was working hard at the same time on the early stages of *Aurora Leigh*. She told Arabel about the daily schedule: 'We are up early, working, working. Penini's lessons I never neglect – then I write. – Then dinner – then I criticize Robert's manuscripts. Altogether I have scarcely breath for reading.' When not being taught by his mother or father, Pen was mainly in the care of Elizabeth Wilson, his beloved 'Lily'. It was a condition of her job to leave her own child behind in England with relatives soon after his birth in 1855. This has caused understandable outrage in recent years, although it is dangerous to apply modern standards too rigorously in mid-nineteenth-century contexts. It is perhaps some consolation to be able to report that Browning later paid Wilson a generous pension and that Pen brought both his old nurse and her husband Ferdinando Romagnoli, who had also been employed at Casa Guidi, to live with him in their old age.

The title *Men and Women* may refer to Browning's contention, in his second letter to Barrett, that 'You speak out, *you*, – I only make men and women speak.' In 'One Word More', a final poem added when the rest of the collection was in proof, he presents his poems, full of different people, different voices, 'to E.B.B.', but in so doing 'speaks out': 'Let me speak this once in my true person,/Not as Lippo, Roland or Andrea.' In fact, he speaks out to a fair extent in several other poems in the collection, perhaps most interestingly in the semi-autobiographical 'By the Fireside'. Here the speaker imagines himself by the fire at some future date, 'O'er a great wise book as beseemeth age'. Apparently intent on his Greek, he is actually, in imagination, moving through an 'inside-archway' until 'we slope to Italy at last/And youth, by green degrees'. What follows is both an evocation of a walk with his

the

ome

illy

BY THE FIRE-SIDE.

— ◆ —

1.

How well I know what I mean to do

When the long dark Autumn evenings come,

And where, my soul, is thy pleasant hue?

With the music of all thy voices, dumb

In life's November too!

2.

I shall be found by the fire, suppose,

O'er a great wise book as beseemeth age,

While the shutters flap as the cross-wind blows,

And I turn the page, and I turn the page,

Not verse now, only prose!

beloved in the hills near Bagni di Lucca and a meditation on how their love grew to the point where

> *if I think but deep enough,*
> *You are wont to answer, prompt as rhyme;*
> *And you, too, find without rebuff*
> *Response your soul seeks many a time*
> *Piercing its fine flesh-stuff.*

Originally they 'drew together.../Just for the obvious human bliss', but the unexpected result is a communion which will outlast death. This deeper love developed, almost seemed to be inspired by, the landscape in which they walked. At dusk, as the water slips on over the stones and the planet Venus appears, a 'moment, one and infinite occurs' in which 'We two stood there with never a third'.

> *The forests had done it; there they stood;*
> *We caught for a moment the powers at play:*
> *They had mingled us so, for once and good,*
> *Their work was done – we might go or stay,*
> *They relapsed to their ancient mood.*

In so far as Browning is able to 'speak out', he reciprocates the gift and the sentiments of *Sonnets from the Portuguese*, which he received in this same Bagni di Lucca landscape.

Some loves in *Men and Women* are less happy. The duke and the lady in 'The Statue and the Bust', for instance, allow time and opportunity to slip away – as Browning evidently felt he and Barrett might easily have done. In 'A Lovers' Quarrel' the lovers lived happily, playing, laughing, absorbed in each other, 'three months ago/When we lived blocked-up with snow'; now, as the spring usually associated with lovers begins, the man recalls how a mere 'hasty word' parted them as easily as they had come together. In 'Two in the Campagna' the relationship is apparently more stable, but the speaker yearns for a fuller, more total love. The

Campagna is the area of ruins, wild flowers and 'the endless fleece/Of feathery grasses everywhere' which in the nineteenth century still extended many miles from Rome; the Brownings spent six months in the city in 1853-4. In this poem landscape and thought are even

An early illustration
to Browning's poem
'Two in the Campagna'.
Engraving by
E.A. Goodall in
W.R. Willmott,
The Poets of the
Nineteenth Century,
1857.

The British Library
1347 l10

The champaign with its endless fleece
  Of feathery grasses everywhere !
Silence and passion, joy and peace,
  An everlasting wash of air—
Rome's ghost since her decease.

Such life there, through such lengths of hours,
  Such miracles performed in play,
Such primal naked forms of flowers,
  Such letting Nature have her way
While Heaven looks from its towers.

327

more subtly and intimately combined than in 'By the Fireside'. Desire, like the cobweb threads and grasses and breezes of the Campagna, and like the thought that is so difficult to express in words, is never still, never fixed. In the orange cup of a flower five beetles grope 'blind and green.../Among the honey-meal'; the lovers too have found the 'honey-meal' of mutual love, but, groping blindly like the beetles, cannot quite cope with their passion. There should be something more: 'I would that you were all to me,/You that are just so much, no more.' But fulfilment – including sexual union, although Browning alludes to it with necessary Victorian indirectness – is fleeting; 'the good minute goes' and all that remains is the speaker's perception of 'Infinite passion, and the pain/Of finite hearts that yearn'.

Failure to move the beloved to love is only a symptom of the more general malaise of the painter Andrea del Sarto, who speaks one of Browning's favourite dramatic monologues. The source of 'Andrea del Sarto' is Giorgio Vasari's highly influential sixteenth-century *Lives of the Most Excellent Italian Architects, Painters and Sculptors*, a book Browning had long known and which his wife reports him as being 'fond of digging at' in April 1853. He may have been digging away at this time because the previous month John Kenyon had written to ask him to obtain a copy of the self-portrait of Andrea with his wife Lucrezia in the Pitti Palace. Since this proved too expensive to arrange, Browning sent the poem instead, or so he claimed many years later. Andrea was known, says Vasari, as 'the faultless painter'. He was technically highly accomplished, but, as he is aware in the monologue, lacked the inspirational fire of the great Raphael and Michelangelo. In the portrait, as in his life, 'A common greyness silvers everything'. As is demonstrated by the high, impossible aspirations of less 'faultless' artists, 'a man's reach should exceed his grasp,/Or what's a heaven for?' To Browning imperfection was an essential, even an invigorating aspect of life; once a thing comes to perfection, he felt, it perishes. Andrea addresses his reflections to a Lucrezia who is clearly only half listening. Browning puts the silence – a defining feature of the listener in dramatic monologue – to interesting effect. Andrea knows that Lucrezia's pleasure lies elsewhere – not holding hands with him and looking at the view 'Quietly, quietly, the evening through'. When her so-called 'cousin' whistles, he will let her go.

'Fra Lippo Lippi' was, with 'Andrea', one of Browning's favourite pieces for reading aloud. Lippo, another of Vasari's painters, spends nearly 400 lines fluently, funnily, cajolingly, sometimes more threateningly (he has friends in high places) explaining to a group of Florentine watchmen what he – a monk – is doing one spring night 'at an alley's end/Where sportive ladies leave their doors ajar'. He confesses his fleshly desires, but these are linked, importantly, with his philosophy of art. Where his predecessors have painted ethereal figures, he – praised by Vasari for his truthful and moving portrayal of the emotions – paints the flesh, or 'The shapes of things, their colours, lights and shades,/Changes, surprises.' Men and women, not the unearthly scenes his Prior wants him to produce, are his – and his creator's – subject.

A more complicated churchman is the subject of 'Bishop Blougram's Apology'. Blougram is at least partly a caricature of the Roman Catholic leader Cardinal Nicholas Wiseman, whom Browning, with his Dissenting background, regarded with considerable suspicion. But the poem becomes more than a satire on a worldly prelate. Blougram talks with such skill, gives such plausible reasons for his way of life, so out-talks his listener, anticipating all that can be said against him, that it becomes impossible simply to dismiss him. Browning is not interested in people who are saints or sinners only; for him, as for Blougram, 'Our interest's on the dangerous edge of things./The honest thief, the tender murderer,/The superstitious atheist.'

A very different monologue, exploring a darker, more enigmatic world than that of Blougram or the other speakers in *Men and Women*, is 'Childe Roland to the Dark Tower Came'. Browning himself relished the enigma; the poem came upon him, he said years later, 'as a kind of dream. I had to write it, then and there…I did not know then what I meant beyond that, and I'm sure I don't know now. But I am very fond of it.' Browning's 'childe' or candidate for knighthood is on a quest to find the Dark Tower. His predecessors have already failed, and Roland seems certain to fail too. He travels on through a grey, increasingly hostile landscape which seems to reflect his hopelessness. Harsh, dark dock leaves are so bruised 'as to balk all hope of greenness'; 'one stiff blind horse' (taken, said the author, from a tapestry he owned), with 'every bone a-stare,/Stood stupefied, however he came there:/Thrust out past service from the devil's stud!' Later the scenes become even more nightmarish. As he crosses a black, eddying river, Roland spears what 'may have been a water-rat…/But ugh! it sounded like a baby's shriek.' Beyond the river an engine of torture stands mysteriously and menacingly ready: 'a harrow fit to reel/Men's bodies out like silk'.

Still nothing is explained, no allegorical significance suggested for Roland's journey. No end is in sight; but then he looks up and 'somehow', in spite of the dusk, 'the plain had given place/All round to mountains'. In the true tradition of quest

literature they seem to have come to him, not he to them. How has this happened? 'Solve it, you!' cries Roland, apparently turning, at the end of his tether, on the reader as one more persecutor. And then

> *Burningly it came on me all at once,*
> *This was the place! those two hills on the right,*
> *Crouched like two bulls locked horn in horn in fight;*
> *While to the left, a tall scalped mountain...Dunce,*
> *Dotard, a-dozing at the very nonce,*
> *After a life spent training for the sight!*
>
> *What in the midst lay but the Tower itself?*
> *The round squat turret, blind as the fool's heart,*
> *Built of brown stone, without a counterpart*
> *In the whole world.*

The reader, and presumably Roland, knows no more of the tower's significance than at the beginning of the poem. Night returns, 'The hills, like giants at a hunting, lay,/Chin upon hand, to see the game at bay', and the names and failure of 'the lost adventurers my peers' sound in his ears – 'Lost, lost! one moment knelled the woe of years'. The scene is dramatically set for the end:

> *There they stood, ranged along the hill-sides, met*
> *To view the last of me, a living frame*
> *For one more picture! in a sheet of flame*
> *I saw them and I knew them all.*

But despair does not win. 'And yet,' the poem's final assertion begins, 'Dauntless the slug-horn to my lips I set,/And blew. *"Childe Roland to the Dark Tower came"*.' We do not know exactly what he has achieved, even whether he survives. We are left only with the moment of assertion. 'Childe Roland' has been interpreted as a poem about death or the fear of artistic failure; Browning, on one occasion when he was asked whether the meaning was 'he that endureth to the end shall be saved', agreed – or almost agreed, preserving the enigma – 'Just about that'.

Following page:

Browning in 1855, the year he published Men and Women. *Painting by Dante Gabriel Rossetti.*

Fitzwilliam Museum, Cambridge

Men and Women is Browning's most powerful and various collection. Both he and his wife had high hopes that it would transform his reputation and were frustrated by some less-than-appreciative reviews: 'It is really high time', *The Saturday Review* went so far as to declare, 'that this sort of thing should, if possible, be stopped. Here is another book of madness and mysticism.' George Eliot (Mary Ann Evans) in *The Westminster Review*, on the other hand, praised the poet for his 'robust energy…informed by a subtle, penetrating spirit'. But it was a puzzled, not a dismissive or perceptive response, which elicited from Browning a rare attempt to explain the premises of his art. John Ruskin, art historian, critic, painter, social theorist and campaigner, one of the most influential prose writers of the nineteenth century, had met Browning and was very enthusiastic about a number of his poems. But some of the pieces in *Men and Women* seemed to him 'the most amazing Conundrums that ever were proposed to me'. Always one to try to get to the bottom of things, Ruskin wrote to Browning in December 1855 in the hope of being given some solutions. A week later Browning replied, with a degree of exasperation, that

> *I cannot begin writing poetry till my imaginary reader has conceded licences to me which you demur at altogether. I know that I don't make out my conception by my language; all poetry being a putting the infinite within the finite. You would have me paint it all plain out, which can't be…You ought, I think, to keep pace with the thought tripping from ledge to ledge of my 'glaciers', as you call them; not stand poking your alpen-stock into the holes, and demonstrating that no foot could have stood there; – suppose it sprang over there?*

Such a method works only for prose; with poetry, as Browning conceives it, it is no use expecting 'that a Druid stone-circle' – a Stonehenge – 'will be traced for you with as few breaks to the eye as the North Crescent and South Crescent that go together so cleverly in many a suburb'. It is not the poet's business to tell people 'what they know already, as they know it…Do you think people understand *Hamlet*?'

October 185

≈ *Paris and London*

W hen *Men and Women* was published, in November 1855, the Brownings were living in Paris during their second long visit to France. Between July and October they had been in London, again seeing a long list of friends. There they breakfasted with Kenyon in order, Barrett Browning said, to meet 'half America and a quarter of London': her work was already popular in America and Browning's was becoming so. Many of the couple's friends in Italy were Americans, among them the

*The Brownings'
address book, compiled
mainly by Browning
in the 1850s. Dante
Gabriel Rossetti and
John Ruskin are listed
near the top of this
page.*

*The British Library
Ashley MS 5718 f45*

sculptor William Wetmore Story, who, in August 1861, wrote to his friend Charles Eliot Norton that 'Browning is not by nature an Englishman', for 'Englishmen who think are very rare; they are generally ganglions of prejudices, which they call opinions'. (This, the Brownings would no doubt have agreed, was why so few of their reviewers seemed to know what they were talking about.)

About ten days after breakfast at Kenyon's they met an American whom Browning found distinctly less congenial – the spiritualist medium Daniel Dunglas Home (pronounced 'Hume'). 'Manifestations' at Home's séances were the talk of fashionable London. Spiritualism was popular because of charismatic mediums like Home and, more broadly, because of the erosion of more traditional religious beliefs. It attracted numerous well-connected adherents, including the author and politician Edward Bulwer-Lytton and the novelist Harriet Beecher Stowe. Elizabeth Barrett Browning was highly interested in this 'table-turning' craze – the spirits or the mediums often made tables move – and rather easily persuaded by it. In Florence many friends, including Alfred Tennyson's brother Frederick, shared her keenness. But her husband emphatically did not. He was convinced on the whole – rightly, it would seem, in many cases – that the mediums were frauds; it was up to them to prove otherwise. Anne Thackeray, the novelist's daughter, records that Browning was always 'irritated beyond patience' when the subject came up in company. 'I can remember [Barrett Browning's] voice, a sort of faint minor chord, as she, lisping the 'r' a little, uttered her remonstrating 'Robert!' and his loud, dominant baritone sweeping away every possible plea she and my father could make.' He was particularly angry about the Home séance they went to, where an alleged spirit hand had placed a wreath of clematis on Barrett Browning's head. Later Home would claim that Browning was simply piqued that the hand had not crowned him. When Home had the temerity to visit a few days later, Browning, to his wife's consternation, threatened to throw the medium downstairs if he did not rapidly remove himself. (People often commented on his general physical energy – striding about the room while Barrett Browning remained calmly sitting.) In the long term, he resorted not to violence but to poetry: Home is the main inspiration for the cunning, resourceful, mock-repentant speaker of his long dramatic monologue 'Mr Sludge, 'the

Medium" in *Dramatis Personae* (1864), probably written mainly in 1859–60 but not shown to his wife.

Spiritualism remained a sore point between the Brownings. They also disagreed, if less violently, over the embroidered dresses, ribbons and long curls worn by Pen at his mother's insistence. But it is clear that in most respects the marriage continued happy, as did the working relationship (they laboured hard on each other's proofs). One occasion they both particularly enjoyed in London was the evening of 27 September 1855, when, in the apartment they were renting at 13 Dorset Street, Tennyson read his *Maud* and Browning his 'Fra Lippo Lippi'. The small private audience included Arabel Barrett, Sarianna Browning, and the poet and painter Dante Gabriel Rossetti, who gave posterity at least some sense of the look of this 'night of the gods' by surreptitiously sketching the poet laureate in full flow. Barrett Browning's letters to Henrietta and others describe talk, port, smoking (one of Tennyson's most passionate enthusiasms), poetry and going to bed at three in the morning – a far cry from her reclusive younger days. (One might wonder why she didn't read aloud like the others. Apart from what she and they may have considered acceptable for a woman on such occasions, she had, by all accounts, a weak voice and a quiet public demeanour.) The sketcher's brother, William Michael Rossetti, left the fullest later accounts of the readers' contrasting approach: Tennyson's 'grand deep voice sways onward with a long-drawn chaunt, which some might deem monotonous, but which gives noble value and emphasis to the metrical structure and pauses', while Browning 'took much less account of the poem as a rhythmical whole; his delivery had more affinity to that of an actor, laying stress on all the light and shade of the composition – its touches of character, its conversational points, its dramatic give-and-take'.

Moving on to Paris, they continued to receive many visitors, at first in a rather cramped apartment to whose yellow sofas they took a particular dislike, and then in more comfortable accommodation at 3 rue du Colisée. They also saw Browning's father and sister regularly. Barrett Browning enjoyed the city, which she was soon to write about in Book Six of *Aurora Leigh*: 'The glittering boulevards, the white colonnades/Of fair fantastic Paris' which Baron

I hate the dreadful hollow behind the little wood

Haussmann was creating as a showcase for Napoleon III's regime. Browning enthused knowledgeably about Italian art when he took Dante Gabriel Rossetti around the Louvre, walked the boulevards and cemented his reconciliation with Macready by going to the theatre with him and Charles Dickens.

In June 1856 the Brownings visited London again. John Kenyon, with his usual generosity, lent them his house at 39 Devonshire Place. Edward Barrett, equally true to form, responded to news of their arrival by banishing Arabel and several of her brothers to Ventnor, on the Isle of Wight. (Alfred Barrett, like Elizabeth and Henrietta, had now married and been disinherited.) The Brownings followed in August; they were anxious to visit Kenyon, who was also on the island, terminally ill. By the time he died in December, the Brownings had returned to Italy, fleeing the effects of northern fogs on Barrett Browning's lungs. There they learnt that their old benefactor, whom Browning once declared should be called 'Kenyon the Magnificent', had performed one final service for them. Since Pen's birth he had been sending them a useful £100 a year. Now he left £6,500 pounds to Browning and £4,500 to Barrett Browning – the division reflecting Browning's more scanty funds. They had achieved lasting financial security.

Kenyon lived just long enough to read the dedication to him of *Aurora Leigh*, a last 'poor sign of esteem, gratitude, and affection from your unforgetting E.B.B.' She ventures 'to leave in your hands this book, the most mature of my works, and the one into which my highest convictions on Life and Art have entered'. Her earlier dedications had been to her father; Kenyon, both as a supportive older kinsman and a literary adviser, had proved a worthy replacement.

Aurora Leigh

Barrett Browning began writing *Aurora Leigh* in earnest in 1854, although as long ago as 1844–45 she had been telling Mitford and Browning about a possible 'sort of novel-poem' which would tell a story and, again like the Victorian

A page from an early draft of Barrett Browning's Aurora Leigh *in which the heroine is called 'Aurora Vane'.*

Wellesley College Library, Special Collections

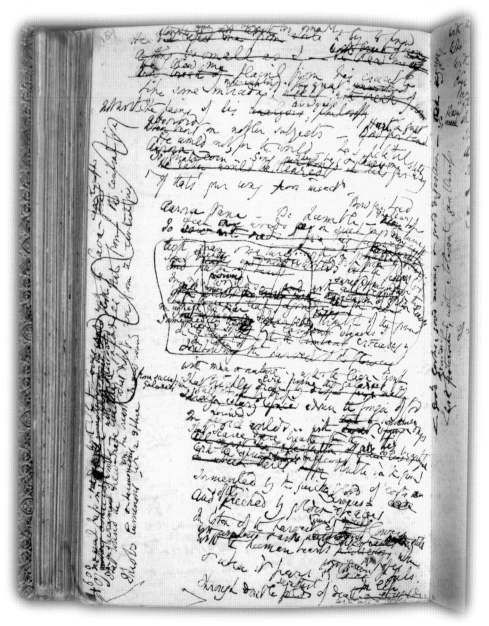

novel, deal with 'this real everyday life of our age' while allowing 'as much philosophical dreaming and digression…as I like to use'. Work ground to a halt in the busy summer and autumn of 1855, but in Paris between December of that year and June 1856 she wrote hard to complete the 11,000-line poem. While Browning needed to write in perfect quietness, his friend Alexandra Orr records that Barrett Browning

> *wrote in pencil, on scraps of paper, as she lay on the sofa in her sitting-room, open to interruption from chance visitors, or from her little omnipresent son; simply hiding the paper beside her if anyone came in, and taking it up again when she was free.*

Aurora Leigh takes the form of an autobiography by a young writer, born in Italy to a loving Italian mother and English father. After her parents' death she is taken, at thirteen, to be brought up by her emotionally repressed aunt in England. Unloving but dutiful, her aunt educates her in the ways of the English gentlewoman. She must read the right religious teachings and tracts, learn languages and a little mathematics and less science (just enough not to appear 'frivolous'), and know how to perform unimaginative musical feats. She does decorous sketches of sea-nymphs 'neatly draped', dances, stuffs birds and models flowers in wax because her aunt 'liked accomplishment in girls'. She reads conservative books on womanhood – many were available in the 1850s – which 'boldly assert' women's

> *right of comprehending husband's talk*
> *When not too deep, and even of answering*
> *With pretty 'may it please you,' or 'so it is'.*

This sarcastic catalogue of conventional female education is one of the first samples of the wittily inventive, highly articulate 'philosophical dreaming and digression' of *Aurora Leigh*. In spite of her aunt, Aurora maintains her inner life, reads widely, learns to enjoy English landscape and becomes a poet.

During the course of the poem, the heroine encounters a wide range of English social types, from the cynical and conniving aristocrat Lady Waldemar to the poor seamstress Marian Erle. (Readers have, however, often objected to the contrast between good-hearted Marian and the generalized violent, drunken degradation of other working-class characters in the poem.) All three women are linked by their interest in, or involvement with, Aurora's rich cousin Romney Leigh. Romney, a Christian socialist, is certain that he can transform the lives of the poor, and equally certain that Aurora should marry him and help him in this work. She refuses because, as she tells him, his true love is 'not a woman…but a cause:/You want a helpmate, not a mistress, sir'; he is wedded to his social theory. Subsequently, as if to prove her point, he decides to marry Marian Erle, not because he loves her but to demonstrate his opposition to class distinctions (and to obtain a suitable helper). He 'lives by diagrams', Aurora reflects, and 'crosses out the spontaneities/Of all his individual, personal life/With formal universals'. Instead of marrying him, she makes a career as a writer. Barrett Browning named her after one of the independent women she most esteemed – George Sand, whose real first name was Aurore.

Aurora herself must unlearn some theories before the end of the poem. As a result of a complex and at times rather melodramatic series of events, Marian does not marry Romney, ending up instead in Paris where, a victim of rape, she gives birth. It is when she hears the details of Marian's story – how she was 'not ever, as you say, seduced,/But simply, murdered' – that Aurora unlearns her conventional condemnation of Marian for having a child out of wedlock. She is persuaded – shocking many contemporary readers – that Marian is in the true sense 'pure'. (There was still much outrage when, in 1891, Thomas Hardy gave the subtitle 'A Pure Woman' to his novel about another victim of male sexual violence, *Tess of the D'Urbervilles*.) Aurora decides that she, Marian and the child will set up house together in a villa on the hill of Bellosguardo (where the Brownings' friend Isa Blagden lived), above olives, maize, vines, cypresses, and Florence with its towers, palaces and 'river trailing like a silver cord'. Florence is a place of homecoming for Aurora and for Barrett Browning, of home-making for Marian, no longer duped, ostracized or living primarily in relation to men. The common notion of the time that unmarried mothers must be punished, cannot be true mothers, is rejected, as Aurora rejected the proposal of the theoretical Romney.

By the time Romney arrives on Bellosguardo towards the end of the poem, however, he too has become untheoretical enough for Aurora to accept his second proposal. Once he was sceptical about the power of poetry and the very idea of women writing it, but now the failure of his own endeavours and the experience of reading his cousin's mature work have persuaded him otherwise. On the other side, Aurora has come to feel that her poetry and her independent life are not totally fulfilling: 'Art is much, but love is more' and now she tells Romney that she has always loved him.

Some readers find this ending disappointing, a step back from the earlier position that women could flourish independently of men. To some extent it reflects the tradition of happy endings in novels. To a greater extent, however, committed though Barrett Browning was to rights for women, it reflects her fervent belief in the virtues, indeed the holiness, of marriage, or at least the sort of mutual, non-patriarchal marriage she had experienced. And the ending did not prevent the poem from having an immediate impact on more radically feminist readers, including the so-called Langham Place Group, one of whose leaders, Frances Power Cobbe, enthusiastically acknowledged the poem's 'sturdy wrestlings and grapplings, one after the other, with all the sternest problems of our social life'. And of course, as Cobbe was aware, in its epic length and scope *Aurora* attests unequivocally to the ability of women to enter traditionally male preserves. The poem adventurously mixes epic and novel, narrative and satire. It gives an account of 'the growth of a poet's mind' like Wordsworth's *The Prelude*, but one which also focuses much more on social issues, including, like no long poem before it, the position and problems of women.

Concern with such issues in the 1850s marked Barrett Browning's work as modern, particularly when seen in the context of the medieval themes and settings beloved of many of her contemporaries. As Aurora wittily and forcefully declares:

> *I do distrust the poet who discerns*
> *No character or glory in his times,*
> *And trundles back his soul five hundred years,*
> *Past moat and drawbridge, into a castle-court*
> *To sing – oh, not of lizard or of toad*
> *Alive i' the ditch there, – 'twere excusable,*
> *But of some black chief, half knight, half sheep-lifter,*
> *Some beauteous dame, half chattel and half queen,*
> *As dead as must be, for the greater part,*
> *The poems made on their chivalric bones.*

One casualty of such medievalism is a proper attention to modern gender relations – as opposed to those between knights and ladies, or robber barons and their 'chattels'. 'Nay,' Aurora goes on,

> *if there's room for poets in this world (I think there is)*
> *Their sole work is to represent the age,*
> *Their age, not Charlemagne's, – this live, throbbing age,*
> *That brawls, cheats, maddens, calculates, aspires,*
> *And spends more passion, more heroic heat,*
> *Betwixt the mirrors of its drawing-rooms,*
> *Than Roland with his knights at Roncesvalles.*

Aurora was widely reviewed. It was unlike anything the reviewers had read before; most found parts to their liking, but a fair number, affronted by the size and audacity of the undertaking or the sex of the undertaker, judged the whole 'hysterical' or strained. Henry Chorley, for *The Athenaeum*, admitted that the purpose was noble but found the mixing of tones and topics intolerable: 'Milton's organ [epic verse] is put by Mrs Browning to play polkas in Mayfair.' But in The *Westminster Review* George Eliot, just embarking on her career as the most notable female novelist of the second half of the century, saw the mingling much more positively: this is the first work by a woman 'which superadds to masculine vigour, breadth, and culture, feminine subtlety of perception, feminine quickness of sensibility, and feminine tenderness'. The Brownings enjoyed the positive comments and were relatively unsurprised by the objections – particularly the predictable claim that one should not so much as write about the likes of Marian Erle. Altogether, Barrett Browning told Anna Jameson, *Aurora* 'is nearer the mark than my former efforts – fuller, stronger, more sustained'. It was near enough the mark to go through thirteen editions by 1873.

The Brownings in 1859. Crayon drawings by Field Talfourd.

National Portrait Gallery, London

Italy, 1856–61

The Brownings arrived back in Florence at the end of October 1856, two weeks before the publication of *Aurora*. For a time, with the effort of composition, revision and proofs over at last, Barrett Browning was exhausted and ill. With her husband's support, she had managed greatly to reduce her morphine intake, particularly when she was pregnant with Pen, but now she felt – probably correctly – that a regular dose was all that kept her alive. Her spirits were further depressed by her father's death in April 1857; she had still hoped for a reconciliation, and could take only some comfort in his having recently admitted to a friend that he had forgiven his erring children and prayed for their families.

Barrett Browning's drawing of her favourite fig-tree, Siena, 1860. To the right Browning has written, 'Drawn the last time she ever sat under it. We left, the next day'.

The British Library 2725 c264

In spite of her failing health, during the last few years of her life she went on writing hundreds of interesting letters and a good number of poems, and survived an exhausting last visit to France in 1858. She maintained her passionate involvement in Italian politics, and her idealism survived even the shock of Napoleon III's decision to make peace with the Austrians after he and his Piedmontese allies had defeated them in June 1859. When she first heard the news of the Treaty of Villafranca, by which Austria gave up Lombardy but retained Tuscany and the Veneto, her health went into what looked like a final decline. She had fallen, she told Henrietta, 'from the mountains of the moon where I had walked hand in hand with a beautiful dream'. But she soon reasoned herself into believing in the emperor again – the 'Emperor Evermore' of her poem 'Napoleon III in Italy'. In the preface to *Poems Before Congress* (1860, named in anticipation of a congress on Italy which, in the event, failed to take place) she boldly attacked not the emperor or the Austrians but her fellow countrymen, on the grounds that they had failed to do anything to help Italy gain its independence. She may have written 'too pungently' in the Italian cause 'to admit of a patriotic respect to the English sense of such things', but truth, she felt, was more important than country. 'Non-intervention in the affairs of neighbouring states' – Italy, obviously – may be 'a high political virtue; but non-intervention does not mean passing by on the other side when your neighbour falls among thieves.' Predictably, such remarks were not well received by reviewers at home.

Barrett Browning also remained committed to spiritualism. In the summer of 1857 at Bagni di Lucca she met Sophia (Sophie) Eckley, a wealthy American in her mid-thirties. Eckley, aware that Barrett Browning was in a vulnerable state following the death of her father, fabricated or exaggerated spiritualist experiences for her benefit, so successfully that the poet thought of her as her sister 'of the spiritual world'. Eckley also, in her desperate desire to retain Barrett Browning's friendship, showered her with embarrassingly expensive gifts. Their relationship was, for a time, very intimate. Browning, opposed to spiritualism and distrustful of the rather sycophantic Sophie, could make no headway when he tried to warn his wife about her. Only when the Brownings spent the summer of 1859 in Siena, while Sophie and her husband, David, went to Bagni di Lucca, did Barrett Browning begin to realize that she had been lied to. She eased herself, politely but firmly, out of the relationship. There was no open quarrel, partly because the older woman freely blamed herself for being taken in (Browning was not slow to agree) – although she would not give up her faith in the possibility of contact with spirits. But when it became apparent that Sophie Eckley wanted to go on seeing her sometimes only so that other people would think they were still friends, she became angrier and wrote an uncharacteristically personal verse attack, 'Where's Agnes?' Here the superficially sweet and pure Agnes – Sophie in very thin disguise – has proved so false that it would be better to have discovered she had died.

Browning wrote relatively little poetry in the late 1850s, but was generally agreed to be thriving. His wife told their friend Isa Blagden in January 1859 that in Rome he was walking with David Eckley at six o'clock every morning, eating vigorously, and

plunged into gaieties of all sorts, caught from one hand to another like a ball, has gone out every night for a fortnight together, and sometimes two or three times deep in a one night's engagements. So plenty of distractions, and no Men and Women. Men and women from without instead!

In Rome he spent much time drawing and, under the direction of his friend Story, modelling in clay. He had also, with drawing in mind, bought a skeleton in April 1858, which is casually listed, in his account book, now in The British Library, on the same page as 'Ba's bonnet' and 'F's [Ferdinando's] wages'. His wife worried somewhat about his lack of regular application to poetry – 'it wouldn't be right for me, and I heard the other day that it wouldn't be right for Tennyson', she told Sarianna in January 1861 – but she realized that 'the brain stratifies and matures creatively, even in the pauses of the pen'. And during those necessary pauses, he needed to use up – by walking, riding, sculpting, or the 'night's engagements' – his 'enormous superfluity of vital energy'. If that energy 'isn't employed, it strikes its fangs into him…Nobody understands', the letter to Sarianna continues, 'except me who am in the inside of him and hear him breathe. For the peculiarity of our relationship is, that even when he's displeased with me, he thinks aloud with me and can't stop himself.' ('Ba and I know each other for time, and, I dare trust, eternity', Browning wrote to George Barrett a few months later.) This is one reason why no amount of disagreement over Sophie and the spirits, Napoleon III as Messiah or Machiavel, or Pen's extraordinary wardrobe could seriously damage the marriage. It is also fortunate that Barrett Browning was happy for her more energetic and gregarious husband to spend so much time wandering about Florence and Rome without her.

The Brownings stayed in Rome between November 1860 and the beginning of June 1861. As usual, they hoped that the climate – warmer and drier than Florence – would do Barrett Browning good, or at least prevent her health from deteriorating

Barrett Browning and her son, Pen (left), and Robert Browning (right), Rome, 1860. Pen's distinctive clothing was more to his mother's taste than to his father's.

Balliol College, Oxford

further. But she remained very weak, coughed persistently, and was increasingly dependent on morphine. Since the summer of 1860 she had also been desperately anxious about her sister Henrietta, who had uterine cancer. The expected but shattering news of her death on 23 November 1860 reached Rome early in December. And yet still Barrett Browning received some visitors, including Hans Christian Andersen. After meeting him in May 1861 she wrote her last poem, 'The North and the South'. At around the same time, at a children's party given by the Storys, Andersen read his 'Ugly Duckling' and Browning 'The Pied Piper of Hamelin'. In the absence of a piper, Story took up his flute and led the children marching about his spacious apartment in Palazzo Barberini.

The author of *Aurora Leigh* remained alive to social and gender issues: in the spring of 1861 she sent Thackeray, as editor of *The Cornhill Magazine*, her poem 'Lord Walter's Wife', in which a married woman outrages a man's sense of moral decency by talking to him seductively, and then turns the tables by pointing out that

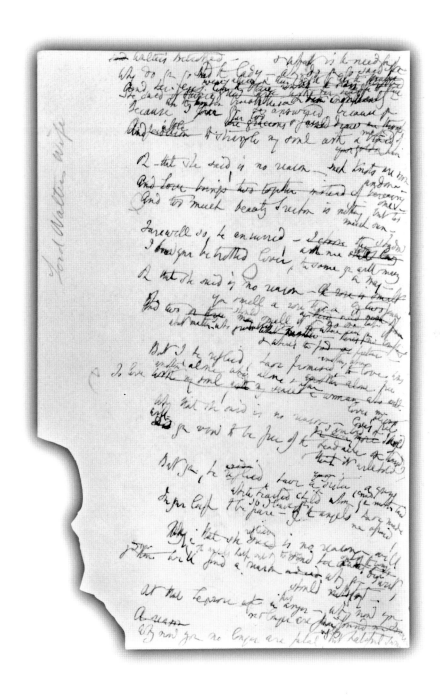

Barrett Browning's draft of her poem about male double standards, 'Lord Walter's Wife'. At this stage the title was 'Walter's Betrothed'.

The Pierpont Morgan Library, New York

he expects to be able to say similar things to her, to claim that she is 'far too fair' and kiss her fan with impunity. Thackeray replied, in a tactful, self-deprecating letter, to the effect that, 'pure' though her poem is, his readers 'would make an outcry' at any account of 'unlawful passion'. He was apologetic. 'Madam, you know how I respect and regard you, Browning's wife and Penini's mother.' Equally polite, but understandably not too impressed by 'your kind way of naming my dignities' as wife and mother, she accepted his excuses but told him, 'I am deeply convinced that the corruption of our society requires not shut doors and windows, but light and air.' ('Lord Walter's Wife' appeared in *Last Poems* in 1862. For *The Cornhill* she sent Thackeray, instead, an uncontroversial poem about a dead child, 'Little Mattie'.)

Early in June 1861 the Brownings travelled back through Siena to Florence, now at last, since March 1860, part of a largely united Italy. The day after their arrival they heard of the sudden death of the architect of this new Italy, the prime minister Count Cavour. Barrett Browning's already fragile health was further damaged by the shock; her passionate hope for the completion of unification and the progress of the new kingdom had been bound up with Cavour. He, not the more charismatic and daring Risorgimento fighter Garibaldi or the idealist Mazzini, had entered the pantheon of her heroes and, to a degree, even become identified with her own continued survival. But the immediate cause of her final collapse was, Browning thought, her insistence on leaving the windows of Casa Guidi open a fortnight later, on 20 June. The sore throat, coughing and breathing difficulties that followed were bad enough, by one o'clock on the morning of 23 June, for Browning to rush off for a doctor. Dr Wilson's poultice and other prescriptions helped to calm the symptoms by daybreak, and at times over the next week the patient said she felt much better. She was sceptical about the diagnosis: Dr Wilson thought she had an abscess on the right lung, but she was sure the problems had always been with the left lung.

Soon after three o'clock on the morning of 29 June Browning noticed that his wife's feet were terribly cold and she talked to him – probably under the influence of an increased morphine dose – about a fine, comfortable steamer she thought she was travelling on. The maid Annunziata (Elizabeth Wilson's successor) bathed her feet in warm water and gave her some jellied chicken. When Browning sent for more water she said – sensing his anxiety, no doubt – 'You are determined to make an exaggerated case of it.' Asked if she knew him, she said, 'My Robert – my heavens, my beloved' and kissed him repeatedly. She told him, 'Our lives are held by God.' He asked if she was comfortable and she replied 'Beautiful.' She seemed to sleep now. He raised her in his arms, where she died at half past four. Annunziata was the first to realize that *Quest'anima benedetta è passata* – 'this blessed soul has departed'.

Elizabeth Barrett Browning was buried at the Protestant cemetery in Florence on 1 July 1861. Shops near Casa Guidi closed as a mark of respect, and many Florentines genuinely mourned the passing of the poet who had spoken so unequivocally on Italy's behalf. William Story wrote to Charles Eliot Norton that the funeral itself was 'not impressive, as it ought to have been' – the service was 'blundered through by a fat English parson in a brutally careless way' – but he did what he could to improve the tone by placing two wreaths on the coffin, 'one of those exquisite white Florence roses, and the other of laurel'.

Elizabeth Barrett Browning's tomb in the Protestant cemetery, Florence. It was designed by the Brownings' friend Frederic Leighton (1830–96), later Sir Frederic and finally Lord Leighton, who became one of the best-known late Victorian painters and sculptors.

The British Library 11612 h2

Robert Browning, 1861–89

Browning's letter to his sister Sarianna, 30 June 1861. Having written the day before to tell her of the death of his wife, he now describes her last days in detail.

British Library MS Ashley 2522 f29b (and A2543)

When Story arrived at Casa Guidi, Browning looked around the room and said, 'The cycle is complete; here we came fifteen years ago; here Pen was born; here Ba wrote her poems for Italy…looking back at these years I see that we have been all the time walking over a torrent on a straw. Life must now be begun anew – all the old cast off and the new one put on. I shall go away, break up everything; go to England and live and work and write.' In preparation for entering English life, Pen had his hair cut and adopted conventional clothing. (Even his mother had agreed that this should happen when he was twelve.)

Robert and Pen Browning, accompanied by Isa Blagden, left Florence on 1 August 1861. Robert Browning found it too painful ever to return. They went first to stay with his father and sister in France. In London they stayed for the first two weeks with Arabel Barrett, whom Browning continued to see frequently until her death in 1868. Her niece, Henrietta's daughter Mary Altham, remembered the two walking around the drawing-room, arm in arm in silent grief. After a period in temporary accommodation, in 1862 Browning took out a lease on 19 Warwick Crescent, his home for the next twenty-five years. Here Pen studied with tutors and with his father, who was keen for him to obtain the formal classical education he had conspicuously done without – Italy was his university, he later told an

American visitor – and to ready himself for the social position Browning's comparative wealth now enabled him to take up. It took the father a long time to accept that the unfortunate Pen's gifts did not lie in the direction of scholarship. He did not, as intended, study at Balliol College, Oxford, under Browning's friend Benjamin Jowett. Even at Christ Church, then regarded as a much less academic college than Balliol, he failed his first examinations – and the re-takes – in 1870. Several years later, however, he was at last able to win the wholehearted approval of his demanding father by embarking on a career as a painter. Although most people felt, and feel, that Pen's work was competent rather than outstanding, Browning did everything he could to promote his reputation. It was Pen, however, who more lastingly influenced his father's – and mother's – reputation by agreeing to the publication of their courtship letters in 1899.

Browning was present when his own father died in Paris in 1866, aged eighty-four. Characteristically, the old man apologized for the trouble he was causing. Browning paid tribute to his memory in a way that neatly illustrates the difference between two parent/child relationships: 'So passed away this good, unworldly, kind hearted, religious man...He was worthy of being Ba's father.' Soon afterwards Sarianna came to live with her brother and nephew.

Robert Browning's home from 1862 to 1887 at 19 Warwick Crescent in London.

Eton College, Windsor

One of the changes in Browning's life after his wife's death was that he began to live and work to a regular schedule. No doubt the aim was originally to keep grief at bay and to set a good example to Pen. In the 1860s he followed much the same regime described, after his death, by William Grove, his manservant between 1875 and 1882. He was up at seven o'clock reading, had a bath at eight, breakfasted at nine, read the newspapers until ten, and wrote in his study until a light lunch at one. With the writing done – Browning always saw it, Pen said later, as a duty, a task to

Browning around the time of the publication of The Ring and the Book. *Photograph by Elliott and Fry, 1868.*

Eton College, Windsor

be got through – he would 'go out to pay afternoon calls or to the private views' of the many painters he knew. At home dinner was at seven o'clock and he went to bed at about eleven. During the London 'season' he dined out most nights but always managed to get up at the same time in the morning. This disciplined approach resulted, of course, in a large body of work, although some of the poems in *Dramatis Personae* (1864), including 'Mr Sludge, the Medium', had their roots in the Italian years.

'Sludge' and two other long monologues in *Dramatis Personae* – 'A Death in the Desert' and 'Caliban upon Setebos' – consider, in their variously oblique ways, the nature of truth, human and religious. Caliban, the denizen of the island in Shakespeare's *The Tempest*, perceives God as the arbitrary Setebos but is also aware of a calmer presence behind him: 'the Quiet'. In the most substantial achievement of Browning's later years, *The Ring and the Book* (1868–9), he explored human perspectives on truth on a larger scale.

This 21,000-line poem again has its origins in Italy. Near the opening Browning describes how, one day in June 1860, he found his main source, 'this square old yellow Book', on a market stall in Piazza San Lorenzo, in Florence, and 'Gave a *lira* for it, eightpence English just'. It consisted of legal documents and pamphlets, most printed in Latin, some hand-written in Italian, connected with the murder by Count Guido Franceschini of his young wife Pompilia and her adoptive parents in Rome in 1698, and the trial and execution of the killer and his accomplices. Murder had fascinated Browning since 'Porphyria's Lover' or before. Particularly interesting was a complex murder case where, although the facts of the crime were not in question, the rights and wrongs of it were. (Guido and his supporters claimed that Pompilia had committed adultery, and desire for money and land motivated some of those involved on both sides.) Browning began reading the book on his way back through the streets to Casa Guidi, but it was not until 1864

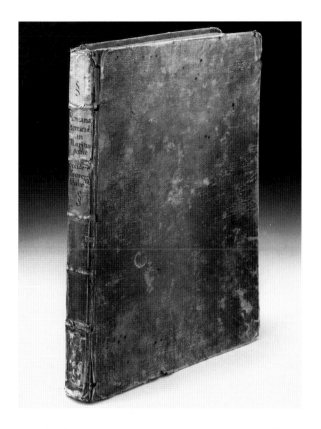

that he began sustained work on the poem. This continued, with some periods of interruption, until 1868.

The story of the murder was one which might, he realized, appeal to a novelist – he offered it to Anthony Trollope, as well as to his fellow poet Tennyson, before taking it up himself – and the fact was further emphasized by the publication of *The Ring and the Book* in four instalments. (Victorian novels usually came out in monthly parts.) Like *Aurora Leigh*, it has some 'novel-poem' elements, including a deep interest both in psychology and in circumstantial detail. But because each of the twelve books contains a monologist's different interpretation of the same apparent facts, *The Ring* seems more modern and unsettling than most contemporary novels. Events are extensively reworked by speakers, including representatives of 'Half-Rome' and 'The Other Half-Rome', who take respectively Guido's and Pompilia's side; Guido, by turns defiant and self-abasing, and then desperate after the verdict; Giuseppe Caponsacchi, the young priest who rescued Pompilia from her husband's tyranny, suspected by some of adultery with her, passionately convinced of her saint-

'The Old Yellow Book' (left), source of Browning's long poem The Ring and the Book, *and Browning's ring, described in the poem. The inscription reads 'Vis Mea' - 'my strength'.*

Balliol College, Oxford

> 1. The Ring and the Book.
>
> Do you see this Ring?
>
>   'T is Rome-work, made to match
> (By Castellani's imitative craft)
> Etrurian circlets found, some happy morn,
> After a dropping April; found alive
> Spark-like 'mid unearthed slope-side figtree-roots
> That roof old tombs at Chiusi: soft, you see,
> Yet crisp as jewel-cutting. There's one trick,
> (Craftsmen instruct me) one approved device
> And but one, fits such slivers of pure gold
> As this was,—such mere oozings from the mine,
> Virgin as oval tawny pendent tear
> At beehive-edge when ripened combs o'erflow,—
> To bear the file's tooth and the hammer's tap:
> Since hammer needs must widen out the round,
> And file emboss it fine with lily-flowers,
> Ere the stuff grow a ring-thing right to wear.
> That trick is, the artificer melts up wax
> With honey, so to speak; he mingles gold
> With gold's alloy, and, duly tempering both,
> Effects a manageable mass, then works.
> But his work ended, once the thing a ring,
> Oh, there's repristination! Just a spirt
> Of the proper fiery acid o'er its face,
> And forth the alloy unfastened flies in fume;
> While, self-sufficient now, the shape remains,
> The rondure brave, the lilied loveliness,

The opening of The Ring and the Book: *Browning's fair copy for the printer.*

The British Library
Add MSS 43485 f1

like purity and innocence; the dying seventeen-year-old Pompilia herself; the satirically presented defence and prosecution lawyers; and the shrewd eighty-six-year-old Pope Innocent XII, deliberating over his refusal of the murderer's appeal although nearly certain of the justice of his decision. Pompilia's innocence remains clear through all this, but it remains equally clear that no individual can judge wholly objectively. In this sense, truth is again 'broken into prismatic hues'.

Through the ring and the book of the title, Browning explores the process (partly mysterious) by which he has transformed the facts of the Old Yellow Book into the different sort of truth contained in the poem. The ring in question was made in Rome for Browning and signifies, for the poet, completeness or perfection; yet just as the finished, carefully shaped poem originated from a looser collection of documents, the ring was once an unformed sliver of pure gold, a 'mere oozing from the mine'. The transformation was made possible by the inspiration of the poet's 'Lyric Love', addressed at the end of Book One and at the end of the whole poem.

Dramatis Personae had sold well and received friendly notices, as had the 1863 edition of Browning's *Poetical Works*. Now, at last, *The Ring and the Book* was generally acclaimed. One reason for this new popularity was his increasing prominence in English society. He was helped also by a change of publisher in 1866: George Murray Smith, of Smith, Elder, promoted his work more effectively than

Chapman & Hall ever had. According to *The Fortnightly Review* 'a striking human transaction has been seized by a vigorous and profound imagination' and 'its many diverse threads have been wrought into a single rich and many-coloured web of art'. One private dissenter from this view was Browning's correspondent Julia Wedgwood, who was perturbed by the preponderance of evil, of 'what is merely hateful'; but crime, of course, has always been popular with readers.

At least as keen a topic of conversation as *The Ring and the Book* was, in many circles, whether the author would re-marry or stay loyal to the memory of his 'Lyric Love'. Julia Wedgwood had reluctantly stopped seeing him in 1865 because, she said, their relationship was being misinterpreted. She was evidently attracted to him and remained a close correspondent for several years. Serious, unworldly, and mourning a brother, she was not unlike the Miss Barrett of 1845. Browning was wounded by her decision to end their meetings, but seems unlikely to have desired more than a spiritual friendship.

He did, however, clearly consider marrying Louisa, Lady Ashburton, a rich widow in her early forties, whom he had first met in 1851. In late August and early September 1869, when he and Sarianna were among the guests on her country estate at Loch Luichart for three weeks, he came to know her better. But whereas it was long believed – it was the impression Ashburton herself gave – that Browning proposed marriage to her, it has now been established beyond reasonable doubt that she proposed to him. Although the details are uncertain, we know that at least the possibility of a marriage was raised at Loch Luichart in 1869 and probably again just over two years later when, it seems, Browning caused Ashburton deep offence by telling her that his heart was buried in Florence and that the only benefit of marrying her would have been the advantages (social and financial, presumably) that would have accrued to Pen. There was no reconciliation. 'Every now and then,' he wrote to Story in June 1874, he saw 'that contemptible Lady Ashburton' and took no more notice of her 'than any other black beetle – so long as it don't crawl up my sleeve'. Browning continued to have many female friends, the closest of whom was Alexandra Orr. It would not have done for the gossip-makers to see, among the gas bills, servants' wages and travelling expenses of his account book for 1877, the sum of

Louisa, Lady Ashburton (1827–1903), who proposed marriage to Browning probably in 1869 or 1871.
Oil painting by Sir Edwin Landseer, 1862.

The Marquess of Northampton

£3.10s spent on 'Ring for A[lexandra].' But he never repeated the uncomfortable sort of involvement he had with Asburton.

The angry aristocrat was not the only person who found it difficult to know Browning's real thoughts and intentions. Those who met him between the 1860s and 1880s were often puzzled, fascinated or deeply disappointed by the gap between his public manner and his poetry. Many people had the opportunity to judge, since during this period he attended an extraordinary number of dinners and parties. Here he met friends and acquaintances, including virtually all his famous contemporaries – prime ministers, diplomats, musicians, novelists, financiers, painters, generals, dukes. (On 12 January 1876 he went for a walk during the course of which he saw and talked with Gladstone, Trollope, the historian Lord Acton and the attorney-general Lord Coleridge.) In company he was very rarely persuaded to discuss his work, preferring to speak volubly on general and, some felt, trivial subjects. All agreed that his public voice was loud; some found it 'resonant' and his manner 'cordial', while others agreed with Gladstone's daughter Mary, who recorded in her diary in 1877 that 'old Browning talks everybody down with his dreadful voice, and always places his person in such disagreeable proximity with yours and puffs and blows and spits in your face'. Julian Hawthorne, son of the novelist Nathaniel Hawthorne, was frustrated by the contrast between the vigorous, impulsive, genial man he remembered from childhood and the 'carefully barbered', expensively and fashionably dressed figure he knew in London in the late 1870s and early 1880s: 'staid, grave, urbane, polished; he was a rich banker, he was a perfected butler, no one would have suspected him of poetry'.

Alexandra Orr, in her *Life and Letters of Browning*, explains very plausibly Browning's own conviction that the loud voice and 'effusiveness of manner' originated principally in a fear of seeming cold to anyone he met and a desire not to pose 'as a man of superior gifts'. And William Rossetti, who watched him for years and carefully analysed his appearance and manner in a series of articles on 'Portraits of Robert Browning' in 1890, suggests that 'one felt his mind to be extraordinarily rich, while his facility, accessibility, and *bonhomie*, softened but did not by any means disguise the sense of his power'. He saved the power itself for his work; when reading it aloud to small, intimate groups, Rossetti says, his 'utterance' even subsided sometimes 'into a tremulous softness which left it scarcely audible'. It seems that in the 1860s Browning built for himself, consciously or unconsciously, an outer shell – a social carapace to cover grief, loneliness and perhaps a degree of uncertainty as he launched himself, apparently so surely, back into English life. However it came about, Henry James (a keen Browning-watcher in the 1870s and 1880s, and a near-neighbour after Browning moved to 29 De Vere Gardens in 1887) had ample grounds for his assertion that he 'had arrived somehow, for his own deep purposes, at the enjoyment of a double identity', had 'literally mastered the secret of dividing the personal consciousness into a pair of independent compartments'. He lived 'almost equally on both sides' of the division. 'It contained an invisible door through which, working the lock at will, he could softly pass and of which he kept the golden key – carrying the same about with him even in the pocket of his dinner-waistcoat, yet even in his most splendid expansions showing it, happy man, to none.'

There are a few known occasions on which Browning did show his deeper feelings in public. His relationship with his old friend John Forster was often uneasy; they quarrelled and were reconciled three times before Forster's death in 1876. Their last estrangement began after Forster had expressed doubts about the veracity of a respectable aristocratic lady. The poet suddenly 'became very fierce, and said, "Dare to say one word in disparagement of that lady" – seizing a decanter while he spoke – "and I will pitch this bottle of claret at your head".' (The incident was recorded by Browning's friend Frederick Lehmann.) In 1884, according to one account, he broke down and wept when the Grosvenor Gallery initially rejected a statue by Pen.

In 1889, the last year of his life, he was – not surprisingly – moved to fury when he came across a casual remark of 1861 in the posthumously published *Letters and Literary Remains* of the poet and translator Edward FitzGerald: 'Mrs Browning's Death is rather a relief to me, I must say; no more Aurora Leighs, thank God!' At once he dispatched a vituperative poem for publication in *The Athenaeum*, wondering whether, if the offender were still alive, he would kick him or do him the grace to spit in his face: 'Spitting – from lips once sanctified by Hers.' There is some evidence that

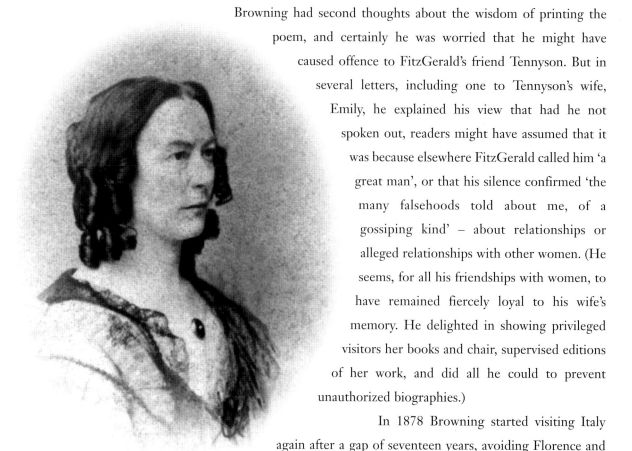

Sarianna Browning, sister of the poet and his loyal companion in early and later life.

Balliol College, Oxford

Browning had second thoughts about the wisdom of printing the poem, and certainly he was worried that he might have caused offence to FitzGerald's friend Tennyson. But in several letters, including one to Tennyson's wife, Emily, he explained his view that had he not spoken out, readers might have assumed that it was because elsewhere FitzGerald called him 'a great man', or that his silence confirmed 'the many falsehoods told about me, of a gossiping kind' – about relationships or alleged relationships with other women. (He seems, for all his friendships with women, to have remained fiercely loyal to his wife's memory. He delighted in showing privileged visitors her books and chair, supervised editions of her work, and did all he could to prevent unauthorized biographies.)

In 1878 Browning started visiting Italy again after a gap of seventeen years, avoiding Florence and painful memories by concentrating mainly on Venice. Here, as on most of his expeditions to France since the 1860s, he was accompanied by Sarianna, always in the background as far as posterity is concerned, but vital to him as daily companion and supporter. In Venice they met Katharine de Kay Bronson (1834–1901), a very wealthy Bostonian expatriate, who became one of Browning's most devoted friends and admirers. Robert and Sarianna Browning spent much time with her in the 1880s at her palace on the Grand Canal, Ca' Alvisi, and her adjoining Palazzo Giustiniani-Recanati, and in 1889 at Asolo, the hill-town near Venice, where she had a second home. Bronson later wrote articles on 'Browning in Asolo' and 'Browning in Venice' for *The Century Magazine*. In the quiet of Asolo, which he had first visited in 1838 and then not again until 1878, 'he never wearied of gazing from the loggia…and of pointing out sights he had kept clear in his mind while writing *Sordello* and *Pippa Passes*', drove in the country, climbed up to the Rocca (the ruined fortress above the town), read poems aloud and confided to Bronson his ambition 'to write a tragedy better than anything I have done yet'. In Venice too he used his time to the full, ferried by Bronson's gondoliers, walking on the Lido, energetically showing friends the sights, going to operas, plays, dinners, feeding the caged animals in the Public Gardens, and sometimes indulging his 'keen flair for good bric-a-brac' for his London home. In 1888, to his great delight, Pen, who had recently married another wealthy American, Fannie Coddington, succeeded in buying a large palace on the Grand Canal, Ca' Rezzonico.

At home and abroad, Browning also went on writing a considerable amount of poetry – fifteen fresh volumes from *Balaustion's Adventure* (1871) to *Asolando; Fancies and Facts* (1889), including monologues, lyric poems, translations from Greek, meditations on murder, love and ambition, from the weighty and abstruse to the quirkily comical. (Some of this material has been unfairly neglected, but it must be said that it only rarely makes for reading as stimulating as *Men and Women* or *The Ring and the Book*.) At the same time, various collections and selections continued to appear. Individual reviews were mixed, but the poet was now fully established and the poems selling, on the whole, well. There was mirth in some quarters when enthusiasts founded a Browning Society in 1881 along the lines of societies dedicated to his respectably dead predecessors, but he was convinced that sales increased because of it. Some people said he should put a stop to the society, he told its co-founder F.T. Furnivall, but that would be like putting a policeman at the door of his publishers to say, 'If you want to buy one of Mr Browning's books, please don't.' The society also gratified him by organizing several productions of his long-neglected plays.

'Some few' of the poems in *Asolando*, the dedication tells Katharine de Kay Bronson, were written, and all of them revised, 'in the comfort of your presence'. The title derives most obviously from Asolo and, says Browning, from *asolare* – 'to disport in the open air, amuse oneself at random'. Some of the poems are suitably sportive. The prologue, however, reflects on 'the Poet's age', when natural objects no longer seem 'to stand/Palpably fire-clothed'. Instead, the power of fancy is replaced by the power of fact; the lens which once bejewelled each object is replaced by one which reveals its shape 'Clear outlined, past escape,/The naked very thing'. Looking beyond age to death, the epilogue to *Asolando* sees this too in a positive light. Towards the end of his life,

Fifine at the Fair.

1.

O trip and skip, Elvire! Link arm in arm with me!
Like husband and like wife, together let us see
The tumbling-troop arrayed, the strollers on their stage,
Drawn up and under arms and ready to engage!

2.

Now, who supposed the night would play us such a prank?
That what was raw and brown, rough pole and shaven plank,
Mere bit of hoarding, half by trestle propped, half tub,
Would flaunt it forth as brisk as butterfly from grub?
This comes of sun and air, of Autumn afternoon,
And Pornic and Saint Gille whose feast affords the boon—
This scaffold turned parterre, this flower-bed in full blow,
Bateleurs, baladines! We shall not miss the show!
They promenade and pace; they presently will dance:
What good were else i' the drum and fife? O pleasant land of France!

3.

Who saw them make their entry? At wink of eve, be sure!
They love to steal a march nor lightly risk the lure.
They keep their treasure hid nor stall (improvident)
Before the time is ripe, each wonder of their tent—
Yon six-legged sheep to-wit, and he who beats a gong,
Lifts cap and waves salute, exhilarates the throng—
Their ape of many years and much adventure, grim
And grey with pitying fools who find a joke in him.
Or, best, the human beauty, Mimi, Toinette, Fifine,
Tricot fines down if fat, padding plumps up if lean
Ere, shedding petticoat, modesty, and such toys,
They bounce forth, squalid girls transformed to gamesome [boys]

Epilogue. 97.

At the midnight in the silence of the sleep-time,
When you set your fancies free,
Will they pass to where—by death, fools think, imprisoned—
Low he lies who once so loved you, whom you loved so,
—Pity me?

Oh to love so, be so loved, yet so mistaken!
What had I on earth to do
With the slothful, with the mawkish, the unmanly?
Like the aimless, helpless, hopeless, did I drivel
—Being—who?

One who never turned his back but marched breast forward,
Never doubted clouds would break,
Never dreamed, though right were worsted, wrong would triumph,
Held we fall to rise, are baffled to fight better,
Sleep to wake.

No, at noonday in the bustle of man's work-time
Greet the unseen with a cheer!
Bid him forward, breast and back as either should be,
"Strive and thrive!" cry "Speed,—fight on, fare ever
There as here!"

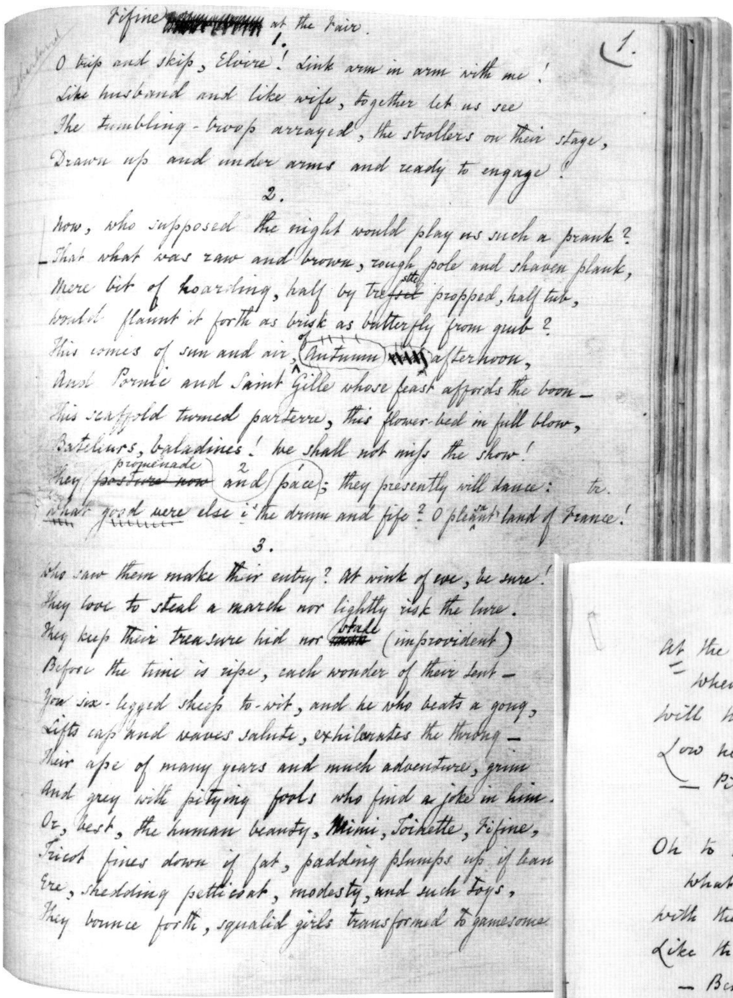

Shown above, the opening of Browning's Fifine at the Fair *(1872), which he told Alfred Domett was his 'most metaphysical and boldest' poem since* Sordello, *and (right) Browning's fair copy for the printer of the epilogue to his last volume,* Asolando *(1889).*

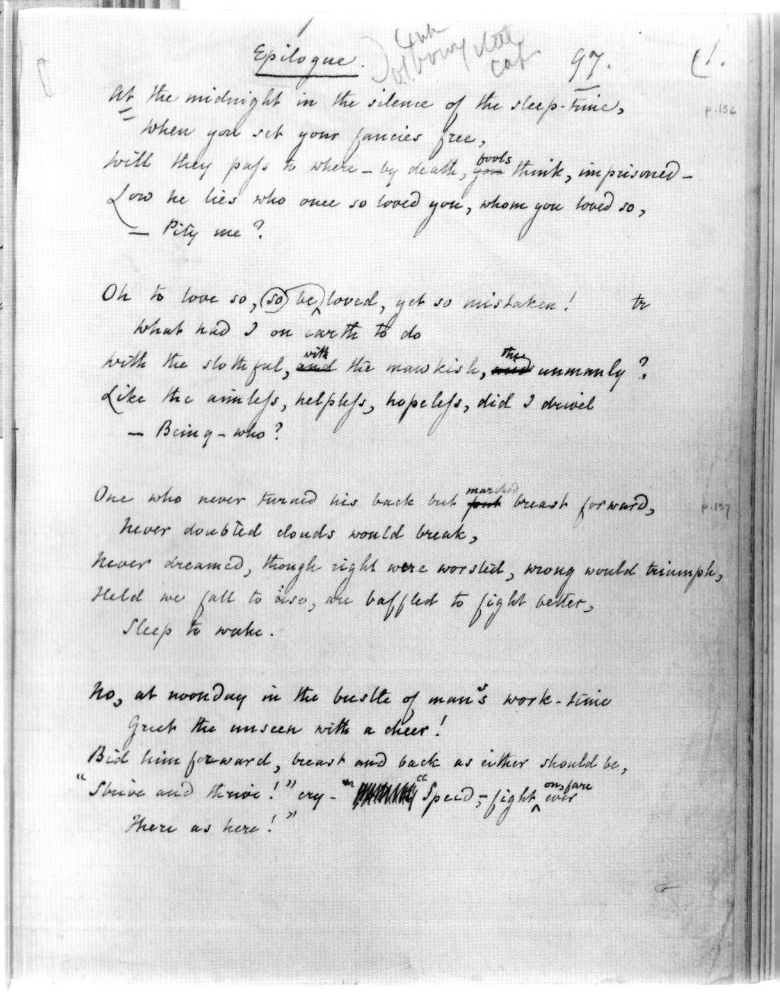

Balliol College, Oxford and The Pierpont Morgan Library, New York

Browning told different people different things about his views on death, assuring some that he was confident of being reunited with his loved ones, admitting to others that he was by no means certain of an afterlife. But in the poem, intended to close what he knew might well be his last work, he both welcomes death and resists association with it: in death no one should pity him, for he was

> *One who never turned his back but marched breast forward,*
> *Never doubted clouds would break,*
> *Never dreamed, though right were worsted, wrong would triumph,*
> *Held we fall to rise, are baffled to fight better,*
> *Sleep to wake.*

When he read these lines to his sister and daughter-in-law from the proof-sheets of *Asolando* in mid-November 1889, Browning was, he told them, 'half ashamed [that they] 'might seem boastful'; but, as F.T. Furnivall reported in *The Pall Mall Gazette* in February 1890, he decided against omitting them because 'it's the simple truth; and as it's true, it shall stand'.

'Mr Robert Browning taking tea with the Browning Society', cartoon by Max Beerbohm.

Ashmolean Museum, Oxford (Copyright the estate of Max Beerbohm, by permission of London Management)

Ca' Rezzonico, the palace on the Grand Canal that Pen Browning bought in 1888 and where Browning died on 12 December 1889. It now houses an important collection of eighteenth-century Venetian art.

The British Library 010827 ee36

Possibly Browning suspected, when he and Sarianna moved on from Asolo to stay at Ca' Rezzonico at the end of October 1889, that he would soon have his chance, as the epilogue puts it, to 'Greet the unseen with a cheer'. But as usual he plunged into the life of Venice, walked on the Lido, went to parties and even read aloud for two hours at the house of some American friends, the Curtises, on 19 November. But two days later he developed bronchitis. He was short of breath, and believed that he was suffering from asthma and a liver complaint. A week later, having sat through a production of *Carmen*, he felt faint on the way up the stairs of Ca' Rezzonico. A doctor was called and it became clear that his heart was failing. A few days later he entered his final decline. At times he was delirious, but in one of the lucid periods, on the morning of 12 December, he was able to look at a newly arrived copy of *Asolando*. In the early evening Pen read him a telegram from the publisher, George Smith, announcing that sales and reviews were both good. 'How

gratifying,' he responded, and added, according to the diary of Evelyn Barclay, a young visitor who had helped nurse him, 'I am dying. My dear boy. My dear boy.' He died at about ten o'clock in the evening.

Browning had said that if he died in England, he should be buried with his mother, if in France with his father, or if in Italy with his wife. Pen, having learnt that the Protestant cemetery in Florence was no longer open for burials, was happy to accept the Dean of Westminster's offer of a place for Browning among the poets in the Abbey. (The link with Barrett Browning was nevertheless asserted when the choir sang a setting of part of her 'The Sleep', which he had read at her graveside twenty-eight years earlier.) In the meantime, the body was solemnly transported, on a huge decorated barge provided by the Venetian municipal authorities, to the cemetery island of San Michele. A few days later it was taken on to London by train. The great and the good of Victorian England assembled in Westminster Abbey for the funeral; 'in this tardy act of national recognition England claimed her own', declared the poet's friend Alexandra Orr. But Henry James suspected that Browning might not have taken the pomp at face value: this was 'exactly one of those occasions in which his own analytic spirit would have rejoiced, and his irrepressible faculty for looking at human events in all sorts of slanting coloured lights have found a signal opportunity'.

⤳ *Chronology*

1806	6 March: Birth of Elizabeth Barrett Moulton-Barrett, first daughter of Edward Barrett Moulton-Barrett (1785–1857) and Mary Graham-Clarke (1781–1828), at Coxhoe Hall, near Durham
1812	7 May: Birth of Robert Browning, son of Sarah Anna Wiedemann (1772–1849) and Robert Browning (1782–1866) in Southampton Street, Camberwell
1819–26	RB attends Peckham School
1820	EBB's *The Battle of Marathon*
1822	Death of Percy Bysshe Shelley
1824	Death of Lord Byron
1826?	RB's *Incondita*
1826	EBB's *An Essay on Mind with Other Poems*
1828	EBB meets Hugh Stuart Boyd. Death of mother, Mary Barrett
1828–29	RB attends London University
1832	The Barretts leave Hope End and move to Sidmouth
1833	RB's *Pauline*
1834	RB travels to Russia
1835	RB's *Paracelsus*. The Barretts move to London
1836	RB meets the actor William Macready and William Wordsworth. EBB meets Wordsworth and Mary Russell Mitford
1837	RB's *Strafford* published and performed. Victoria becomes queen
1838	RB's first visit to Italy. EBB's *The Seraphim and Other Poems*. EBB moves to Torquay
1840	RB's *Sordello*. EBB's brother 'Bro' drowned. The Brownings move to New Cross
1841	Mitford gives EBB Flush, a spaniel. RB's *Pippa Passes*
1842	EBB returns to London. RB's *Dramatic Lyrics*
1844	EBB's *Poems*. RB's second visit to Italy
1845	Courtship begins (first letter 10 January, first meeting 20 May)
1845–46	EBB writes *Sonnets from the Portuguese*

1846	EBB and RB marry (12 September) and settle in Pisa
1847	They move to Florence. Grand Duke Leopoldo II grants the Florentines the right to form a civic guard. EBB starts writing 'A Meditation in Tuscany'.
1848	Leopoldo grants Tuscany a constitution. Louis Napoleon Bonaparte elected president of the French Republic
1849	Birth of Robert Wiedemann Barrett Browning ('Pen'). Death of Sarah Anna Browning. Leopoldo flees, Tuscan republic set up; Leopoldo restored by Austrian troops
1850	RB's *Christmas-Eve and Easter-Day*. EBB's Poems (including *Sonnets from the Portuguese*). Wordsworth dies. Alfred Tennyson succeeds him as poet laureate
1851	EBB's *Casa Guidi Windows*. Coup d'état by Louis Napoleon Bonaparte
1851–52	Extended visit to France and England
1852	Bonaparte becomes Emperor Napoleon III
1855	RB's *Men and Women*
1855–56	Second extended visit to France and England
1856	EBB's *Aurora Leigh*. Death of John Kenyon, who leaves the Brownings £11,000
1857	Death of Edward Moulton-Barrett
1857–59	EBB's friendship with Sophie Eckley
1859	French and Piedmontese victories against the Austrians at Magenta and Solferino. Treaty of Villafranca
1860	Tuscany becomes part of the new kingdom of Italy. EBB's *Poems before Congress*. Death of EBB's sister Henrietta
1861	Death of Count Cavour. Death of EBB (29 June). RB and Pen go to live in London
1862	EBB's *Last Poems* published
1864	*Dramatis Personae*
1866	Death of Robert Browning, senior
1868–69	*The Ring and the Book*

1869?   RB receives proposal of marriage from Lady Ashburton

1872   *Fifine at the Fair*

1878   RB's first visit to Italy since 1861

1881   Browning Society founded

1889   *Asolando.* Death of RB (12 December)

1899   Publication of the courtship correspondence

1903   Death of Sarianna Browning

1912   Death of Pen Browning

Further Reading

Poems

The Works of Elizabeth Barrett Browning (Wordsworth Editions, Ware, 1994)

Aurora Leigh, ed. Margaret Reynolds (Ohio University Press, Athens, Ohio, 1992)

Robert Browning: the Poems, eds. John Pettigrew and Thomas J. Collins
(Penguin, Harmondsworth, 1981)

The Ring and the Book, ed. Richard D. Altick (Penguin, Harmondsworth, 1971)

Letters

The Brownings' Correspondence, eds. Philip Kelley, Ronald Hudson and Scott Lewis
(Wedgestone Press, Winfield, Kansas, 1984–)
The fourteen volumes published so far contain correspondence to the end of 1847.

The Letters of Elizabeth Barrett Browning to Mary Russell Mitford 1836–1854,
eds. Meredith B. Raymond and Mary Rose Sullivan
(Armstrong Browning Library, Waco, Texas, 1983)

More than Friend: the Letters of Robert Browning to Katharine de Kay Bronson,
ed. Michael Meredith (Armstrong Browning Library, Waco, Texas, and
Wedgestone Press, Winfield, Kansas, 1985)

Biographies

Margaret Forster, *Elizabeth Barrett Browning: a Biography* (Chatto & Windus, London, 1988)

John Maynard, *Browning's Youth* (Harvard University Press, Cambridge, Massachusetts, 1977)

Clyde de L. Ryals, *The Life of Robert Browning: a Critical Biography*
(Blackwell, Cambridge, Massachussets and Oxford, 1993)

William Irvine and Park Honan, *The Book, the Ring, and the Poet: a Biography of Robert Browning*
(Bodley Head, London, 1975)

Donald Thomas, *Robert Browning: a Life Within Life* (Weidenfeld & Nicolson, London, 1982)

Julia Markus, *Dared and Done: the Marriage of Elizabeth Barrett and Robert Browning*
(Bloomsbury, London, 1995)

Daniel Karlin, *The Courtship of Elizabeth Barrett and Robert Browning*
(Oxford University Press, Oxford, 1985)

Martin Garrett, ed., *Elizabeth Barrett Browning and Robert Browning: Interviews and Recollections*
(Macmillan, Basingstoke, and St Martin's Press, New York, 2000)

Martin Garrett, *A Browning Chronology: Elizabeth Barrett and Robert Browning*
(Macmillan, Basingstoke, and St Martin's Press, New York, 2000)

Other Important Studies

Marjorie Stone, *Elizabeth Barrett Browning* (Macmillan, Basingstoke, 1995)

Angela Leighton, *Victorian Women Poets: Writing Against the Heart*
(Harvester Wheatsheaf, New York and London, 1992)

John Woolford and Daniel Karlin, *Robert Browning* (Longman, London, 1996)

Boyd Litzinger and Donald Smalley, eds., *Robert Browning: the Critical Heritage*
(Routledge, London, 1968, 1995)

≋ *Index*

The British Library is grateful to the Ashmolean Museum, Oxford; Balliol College, Oxford; The Bridgeman Art Library; Columbia University Libraries; Eton College, Windsor; Fitzwilliam Museum, Cambridge; The Marquess of Northampton; Mill College, California; The National Portrait Gallery; The Pierpont Morgan Library, New York; South Place Ethical Society; The Tate Gallery; The Victoria & Albert Museum; Wellesley College Library and other named copyright holders for permission to reproduce illustrations.

Front cover illustrations:	View of Florence from the Boboli Gardens by Jean Baptiste Camille Corot, The Bridgeman Art Library; 'How do I love thee' from *Sonnets from the Portuguese*, Add MS 43487 f.49, The British Library; Portraits of Elizabeth Barrett Browning, 11612 h.2, and Robert Browning 10203g 3, The British Library.
Back cover illustrations:	Elizabeth Barrett Browning, Balliol College, Oxford; Robert Browning, courtesy of Eton College, Windsor. Coxhoe Hall by courtesy of Robin Walton.
Half title page:	Portraits of Elizabeth Barrett Browning, 11612 h.2, and Robert Browning 10203g 3, The British Library.
Frontispiece:	'How do I love thee' from *Sonnets from the Portuguese*, Add MS 43487 f.49.
Contents page:	Florence from Ponte Vecchio by Giovanni Signorini. The Bridgeman Art Library/Gavin Graham Gallery, London.

I should like to thank Lara Speicher and Kathleen Houghton of the British Library Publishing Office, whose insight and hard work have contributed so much to this book and to my *Byron* in the same series. I should also, as usual, like to thank my family, Helen, Philip and Edmund, for their continuing help and support.   *Martin Garrett*

First published in 2001 by

The British Library

96 Euston Road

London NW1 2DB

British Library Cataloguing in Publication Data

A catalogue for this title is available from The British Library

ISBN 0 7123 4715 1

Designed and typeset by Crayon Design, Stoke Row, Henley-on-Thames

Map by John Mitchell, Colour and black-and-white origination by Crayon Design and

South Sea International Press, Printed in Hong Kong by South Sea International Press